EDITOR: Maryanne Blacker
ASSISTANT EDITOR: Beverley Hudec

• • •

ART DIRECTOR: Paula Wooller
DESIGNER: Robbylee Phelan

• • •

STYLISTS: Karen Byak, Georgina Dolling,
Judy Newman
PHOTOGRAPHERS: Joseph Filshie, Andre Martin,
Rodney Weidland

• • •

ILLUSTRATIONS: Sandy Cull

SUB-EDITOR: Lynn Humphries

• • •

ACP PUBLISHER: Richard Walsh

ACP ASSOCIATE PUBLISHER: Bob Neil

• • •

Produced by The Australian Women's Weekly Home Library.
Typeset by ACP Colour Graphics Pty Ltd. Printed by Dai
Nippon Co., Ltd in Japan.
Published by ACP Publishing Pty Ltd, 54 Park Street, Sydney.
♦ **AUSTRALIA:** Distributed by Network Distribution Company,
54 Park Street Sydney, (02) 282 8777.
♦ **UNITED KINGDOM:** Distributed in the U.K. by Australian
Consolidated Press (UK) Ltd, 20 Galowhill Rd, Brackmills,
Northampton NN4 OEE (0604) 760 456.
♦ **CANADA:** Distributed in Canada by Whitecap
Books Ltd, 1086 West 3rd St,
North Vancouver V7P 3J6 (604) 980 9852.
♦ **NEW ZEALAND:** Distributed in New Zealand by Netlink
Distribution Company, 17B Hargreaves St, Level 5,
College Hill, Auckland 1 (9) 302 7616.
♦ **SOUTH AFRICA:** Distributed in South Africa by Intermag,
PO Box 57394, Springfield 2137 (011) 493 3200.
ACN 053 273 546.

• • •

Classic Crafts

Includes index.
ISBN 0 949128 97 X.

1. Handicraft. (Series: Australian
Women's Weekly Home Library).

745.5

• • •

COVER: Main picture: Papier mache dolls, page 76.
Bottom, from left: Quilted cushion, page 82,
Handmade paper, page 122, Marbled eggs, page 86.
OPPOSITE: Handkerchief with lace edging, page 110.
BACK COVER: Raffia hats, page 2.

CLASSIC CRAFTS

Whether you want to make a family heirloom or an inexpensive gift, you'll find a wealth of ideas in this book. Both traditional and contemporary crafts have been included – splendid handmade paper and fine lace edging; a plaited rag rug and a charming stained glass panel; irresistible papier mache dolls and impressive linocuts; a whimsical basket; a spectacular hat box and raffia hat to put in it, to name just a few. Each project has detailed instructions, step-by-step photographs and appropriate diagrams and illustrations. All you have to decide now is which project you want to start first.

Raffia Hats

No-one knows exactly when people first wore hats — they were originally

worn as protection from the elements. Hats made of natural fibres such

as rushes and straws were worn by many of the early civilisations of Asia

Minor and Europe. One early statue of the god Mercury depicted him

wearing a finely plaited straw hat. In Ancient Rome, hat-wearing was

associated with class: Freed slaves wore caps; the ruling classes usually

went bare-headed. From the 1790s, the cabbage tree hat, made from the

cabbage tree palm, became a status symbol for Australian-born settlers.

YOU WILL NEED

Approx 10-12 x 2cm-wide raffia plait (available from good craft suppliers)

Sewing raffia

Darning or canvas sewing needle

Scissors

A twist of seagrass to adjust the size of the completed crown

Cotton herringbone webbing or grosgrain ribbon

Silk flowers

NOTE

■ *Cotton webbing and seagrass twist may be difficult to find in anything but wholesale quantities.*

■ *Instructions are for right-handed people; left-handed version is reversed.*

TERMS

Easing: This means pushing the plait against the direction in which you are sewing. Never push the plait so that it distorts, as this destroys the natural tension of the straw and decreases the hat's ability to hold its shape.

Pulling: More or less as it sounds. This is the opposite of easing and is used to draw the shaper in at various points of the hat-making. You pull to create the crown sides and to make the brim turn up.

2 Begin the centre of the crown by folding the plait 10cm down from the tied-off end and securing this end under the plait so that it is not visible from above. The upper side is the right side of the work.

3 Close the opening of the loop by stitching the sides together between the tied-off end and the fold at the top of the loop. Stitch by pushing the needle through the plait to the other side of the work; bring it back in the same way, imitating the weave of the plait so that your stitching does not show too much on the finished hat.

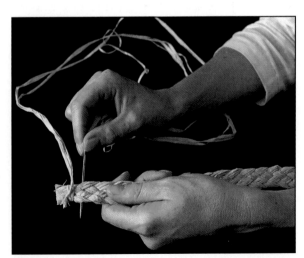

1 To begin, thread your needle with a thread of raffia and, using the unthreaded end, tie off the raw end of the plait securely, but not too tightly – the plait should remain flat. Run the needle through the tied-off section from side to side to secure it firmly, bringing the needle out at the side.

4 When you have closed the loop, push the needle to the wrong side of the work and bring the thread down towards the tied-off end of the loop by catching the back of the work with a stitch.

5 Begin the first turn of the crown by easing the plait around to form an oval. This first turn is tight and you will need to push underneath any little excess bits of raffia that poke up on the turn, or you will get a point on the crown. Stitch this in place neatly and continue around, easing particularly carefully on the ends of the oval to keep the crown centre as flat as possible.

6 Stitch as before by pushing the needle through the plait to the other side of the work and bringing it back in the same way. Take care to ease with every stitch from now on until otherwise instructed. This will prevent the crown from pulling over into a very small dome which will become tighter and tighter, eventually becoming too small to fit your head. Sew around the initial loop twice. You will have a small, flat crown centre with six plait strands, counting from one side to the other.

7 Push the needle through to the wrong side of the work and begin to sew through two strands at once, rather like a flat seam when joining two pieces of knitting; the stitches will not show on the right side. You will be sewing in a clockwise direction. At this stage, you will probably be approaching the end of your first length of sewing raffia. Join a new length by beginning two or three stitches back and sewing over the end to secure it.

Once you have begun sewing through the two strands of plait with one stitch, it is easy to lose control. Be extra careful to continue easing, either keeping the work flat, or allowing a gentle curve to show (depending on how you want the finished hat to look).

Begin the crown sides when you have approximately nine strands sewn from side to side, that is, an oval 22cm x 20cm. You will have sewn around about four and a half times. As plait sizes and head widths vary, you need to be aware that this is the point where you determine the shape of the crown. It is not possible to try the hat on at this stage, so it is best to continue for the next two or three rows of the next stage and then try on the crown. Adjustment can be made at this stage back to the seven to nine rows that you now have. If you make more than one or two hats, you will soon become used to judging the size of the finished crown by the size of the oval at this point.

8 Push the needle through to the right side of the work to begin the crown curve. Your stitches will now be on the outside of the hat. Sew, as before, through two strands at once, using your left hand to pull the plait firmly and to turn it down to form the turn, stitching it in place as you form it. The tension need not to be very tight. It depends to some extent on the plait; however, if the turn is holding and the plait is pulled firmly, you will see the crown forming. The second row should be sewn in the same manner.

9 When the second row is complete, you will have a definite cap which you can try on. It is not easy to judge from this the size of the hat to come, but it's all you have! If the crown cap is enormous on your head, or if it is already fitting perfectly, you may need to unpick or unclip back to the flat oval. Pull harder to make a smaller cap, or much less hard to make it larger. If the cap fits you perfectly at the end of row two of the crown, there is a danger that is going to become too tight in the next row. The perfect fit is slightly big, but not 'swimming'.

Row three should be used simply to deepen the crown. You can ease or pull at this stage, but as you are nearing the end of the crown, you do not want it suddenly tight at this point, because it can form an uncomfortable ridge on your head.

The crown may now be deep enough. If you are using a 2cm plait, you may need one more row. If the plait is slightly wider than 2cm, you will probably have enough depth already. Try on the crown. This is one point where you must judge for yourself. Some people like a very deep crown and others prefer it shallow.

10 To begin the brim you need to find the point at which to roll the plait over at right angles to the crown. To find this point, turn the crown over as if it were a small basket, hold it at eye level, looking along the open edge of the basket, taking care not to tip it to one side. The edges should look the same height at the point at which you are ready to begin the brim.

The hat in the photograph looks lopsided and needs to be sewn a bit further before edges will look even.

Once you get to this even sided point, you need to sew another five or six stitches; these will cause the edge of the crown to become lopsided again. It is this lopsided section which you now fold out at right angles to the crown.

11 Take the needle to the wrong side of the work; that is, the inside of the hat. Turn the crown upwards on your lap and over-stitch the crown and inner brim edge, easing slightly with each stitch to keep the

first row of the brim sitting out flat.

The second row is sewn the same way, easing very slightly to the same degree as the first row. This row should result in the brim beginning to come up into a very slight trumpet shape. This is another danger point. It is easy to find the trumpet becoming too steep too quickly. Easing carefully will prevent this. If, on the other hand, you find that you still have a flat brim, you need to unpick one row without easing. The raffia plait should pull it up without pulling.

In rows three, four and five, there is still a tendency for the trumpet shape to pull up too much and to be too steep. Simply use your eyes to see what it is doing and either ease, sew without easing or even pull, to control the effect.

13 You can choose for yourself how many rows you want on your hat. These instructions take you to row six. The instructions for any additional rows are the same as the first rows. The final row needs some care.

Where the brim was begun – rolling out from the crown – is the point at which you must begin to sew the last 16cm under the brim edge. Find this point at the junction of the crown and brim edge. You will see that the roll begins very slightly. Taking a line straight from here to the outer edge of the brim, begin gradually to sew the plait underneath the brim (that is, the underside of the hat as it sits on your lap, which would be the top side of the brim if you were wearing the hat). This means that when the hat is worn with the brim turned up, the finishing-off tail is hidden on the inside of the turn-up. Continue gradually feeding the plait under the brim, pushing the needle right though from one side to the other, until it is just beyond the edge. Sew it firmly in place and secure it so that it cannot come undone or become frayed. Cut the raffia plait 1-2cm from the end.

Ideally, the hat should feel a little loose on your head. The seagrass twist, when pulled tight around the crown, will adjust the size for a windy day. Finally, tie a bow of black cotton webbing or grosgrain ribbon over the seagrass twist around the crown. For added effect, sew some silk flowers onto the ribbon, positioning them all around the brim, at desired intervals, or in a bunch on one side of the brim.

12 The ideal is an absolutely smooth trumpet mouth for five rows, with the last row – the sixth – being pulled just a little bit at each stitch. This will hold the turn-up of your completed hat. If it flops down, then you need to redo that last row a little more firmly. If the hat is too turned up, then you need to take some of the tension (pulling) out of the last row. Unfortunately, to do this you might possibly have to take one row right off the hat altogether; that is, if you have cut it upon completion. You will find that if you cut the raffia tail off and then need to loosen the outer row, you will not have enough tail left with which to finish off.

Hats in opening photograph by Deborah Wooller.

Linocuts

Printing from linocut blocks is one of several processes known as relief printing. A relief print is made from a raised image which is inked then transferred to paper by applying pressure. The part of the design that is to remain uninked is cut away leaving only those parts to be printed. Because of its nature, lino is best suited to simple designs. Linocutting was very popular earlier this century as a cheap way of bringing modern art to the masses. One protagonist was English artist Charles Flight, whose work attracted an international following during the 1920s and 1930s. Picasso and Matisse were devotees of the linocut movement too.

NOTE

Experiment with different kinds of paper to gauge the effect of the design. A more complex design, such as our doves, looks perfect on heavy, slightly textured paper while a bold, geometric print may really shine on inexpensive coloured cardboard. Be prepared to practise.

Above: Design for a book plate, pictured on previous page.
Below: Design for a greeting card.

YOU WILL NEED

Lino (available from art supply shops)

Linocutting tools (available from art supply shops)

White water-based paint

Flat paint brush

Tracing paper

Carbon paper

Adhesive tape

Sharp knife

Pencil

Bench rest

Washable glass surface on which to roll out ink

Water-based block printing ink (available from art supply shops)

Palette knife

Paper for printing (we used good quality rag-based paper which absorbs ink well)

Two rollers

Burnisher (wooden spoon can be used)

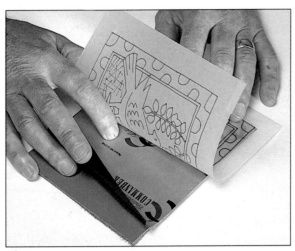

1 Paint the surface of lino with a coat of white water paint. Trace design onto tracing paper.

Place carbon paper ink-side down on top of lino. Place tracing paper design on top. The tracing paper must be laid drawn-side down if the design is to be reproduced the correct way round. This may not matter with some designs, but if letters or numbers are involved, it must be reversed or the final design will be printed back to front. Attach carbon and tracing paper to lino with adhesive tape.

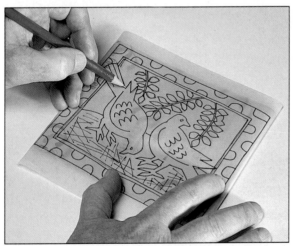

2 Using a pencil, transfer drawing to prepared surface by drawing over the design on the tracing paper. Remove tracing paper and carbon paper from lino.

3 Start cutting out the design. It is a good idea to use a bench rest because this minimises the risk of cuts to the hands. A rest consists of a base with one wooden strip nailed to the top and another nailed underneath to the bottom (see diagram below).

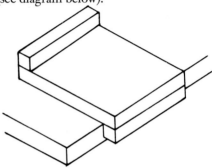

The lino is much easier to cut if it is warmed slightly in front of a heater before beginning work.

Using a small V-shaped cutting tool, cut around outlines of the design. All fine-detailed work should be done with this tool. Remove large areas of lino with a large U-shaped tool.

4 Using a palette knife, mix ink on a clean piece of glass, working it vigorously. When ink is well mixed, ink the roller by rolling it across the glass until roller and glass are evenly coated (this may take a little practice).

5 Transfer the ink to the block, rolling the roller backwards and forwards in different directions (top to bottom, then left to right) to make sure the block is completely covered with ink.

Take a piece of smooth rag-based paper and position it over the block. A textured piece could be used but this will produce a different, much coarser effect.

6 Holding the paper steady, over the block, with one hand, use a clean roller to apply pressure to the paper (this will position the design).

7 Using the burnisher and working from the centre out, systematically apply pressure to the design area of the paper. The roller should not be used at this stage because it will not distribute sufficient paint evenly.

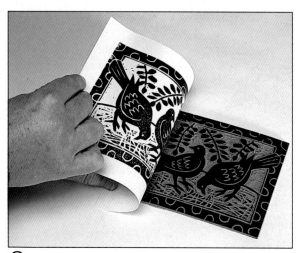

8 To check if you have burnished the paper sufficiently, carefully lift one corner of paper to see if the ink has been properly transferred. If it has not, replace paper and burnish again. Do not remove the paper entirely until you are satisfied. You will not be able to replace it in exactly the same position and will produce a blurred image on the paper.

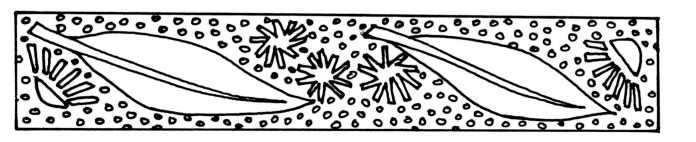

Right: simple motif for adorning stationery. Below: bookmark, design pictured on previous page.

Made by Bill Murphy.

Chapter Four

Three

Months

That Can

Shake

the World

Wreaths

Paper-thin and very fragile flower wreaths have been found in the tombs of wealthy ancient Egyptians. In the days of poor hygiene, flowers were often used in posies and wreaths to ward off infection, promote health and disguise unpleasant odours. These days wreaths are used primarily for decoration: as spectacular table centrepieces, decorative wall pieces or simply sweet smelling additions to a room. We've featured three quite different wreaths: one using dried flowers, one with fresh flowers and the third features fresh kale cabbage leaves and lavender.

Dried Wreath

NOTE

Wiring flower stems. This is sometimes necessary to strengthen a brittle stem or reinforce a stem which is to be pushed into polystyrene or cardboard. Trim stems and bend the wire almost in half. Position wire behind stem and twist one leg of wire twice around stem and other wire leg as shown in diagram. Bend wire end down in line with other wire.

YOU WILL NEED

Branches of fresh crab apple

Bunches of dried miniature red roses (about 40 stems)

Bunches of dried hydrangea (about five heads)

Dried lavender (fresh will droop), without foliage (about 40 stems)

35cm-diameter polystyrene wreath base

18 gauge florist's wire (from florist's or floristry suppliers)

Wire cutters

1 Trim stems of all flowers. Wire lavender and miniature red roses in separate bunches consisting of about five stems each. Wire small bunches of hydrangea. Wire crab apples in bunches consisting of about five or six apples. Do not mix the flowers while wiring.

Beginning at the edge of the wreath on the bottom left-hand side, push in a bunch of crab apples. Place a bunch of lavender slightly above the first, closer to the centre rim of the wreath, then a bunch of roses above that closer to the edge; finally position the hydrangea, working in a herringbone pattern. Continue this around the wreath base, following the direction of the diagram. Fill in the gaps in the wreath base with any leftover bunches to give a full effect.

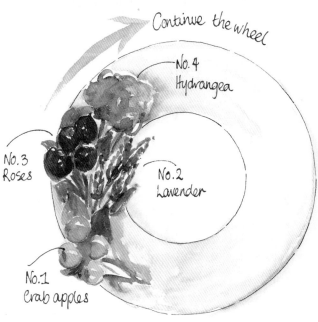

Continue the wheel

No. 4 Hydrangea

No. 3 Roses

No. 2 Lavender

No. 1 Crab apples

Made by Bloomey's, enquiries (02) 360 1788.

Fresh Wreath

NOTE

■ *The flowers used in this wreath do not require wiring.*

■ *If using as a centrepiece, place on a platter or put a plastic underlay under the cloth to avoid watermarks on the table.*

YOU WILL NEED

1 bunch wattle

Leucadendrons (about 12 stems)

Dryandra (about nine stems)

Cardboard-based Oasis wreath base (about 35cm-diameter, available from florist's or floristry suppliers)

1 Dip Oasis in water, invert. Cut all flower stems to required length.

Push wattle stems in around edge of wreath base; this will give you an idea of the size of the finished wreath.

Bunch stems of leucadendron together and stems of dryandra together. Push into wreath; the bunches will add texture.

Add more stems to inside centre of wreath. Fill gaps with wattle and leafy stems.

Kale Wreath

You Will Need

Kale cabbage

Fresh lavender, about 45-50 stems

35cm-diameter polystyrene wreath base (from florist's or floristry suppliers)

18 gauge florist's wire (from florist's or floristry suppliers)

1 Cut wire into 5cm lengths. Bend wire into a half to form a staple shape.

Break leaves away from cabbage. Arrange leaves around the wreath base to get an idea of the design you want.

Beginning at bottom left, place leaves in position on wreath, secure with staple-shaped wire, making sure to overlap leaves so that the wire is covered. Fill in any spaces with extra leaves, making sure to follow the line of the leaves.

Place the centre rose of the cabbage in the bottom centre of the wreath base, secure with wire staple. Fan out the baby leaves from the cabbage around the rose, secure with wire.

Trim lavender stems. Wire bunches, consisting of five stems and three stems, see Note at beginning.

Following the vein of the leaves, place lavender around wreath.

Tie ribbon around top of polystyrene base or secure with wire at back, hang as desired.

19

Combing

The technique of combing is thought to have originated in Ancient Egypt, where leather and wooden combs were used to simulate real wood grain. Combing was also used extensively in European folk decoration in Scandinavia and Germany (early German settlers carried the art to America). Basically, a ribbed or striped combination of two colours is achieved by scraping the teeth of a comb through a surface glaze. It is a decorative and relatively inexpensive finish which is suitable for walls, floors, picture frames and furniture. Designs can be subtle or high in contrast, depending on the way the comb is handled.

You Will Need

Piece of pine furniture
Fine sandpaper
Satin enamel paint (we used pale grey)
Paintbrush
Acrylic paint, (we used yellow)
1m muslin
**Scumble glaze (we used Porters Original
    Limewash Roman green)**
**Combs, wooden, metal, rubber or plastic
    (available from art supply shops)**
Clean, cotton rag
Paint tray
Mineral turpentine
Varnish, matt or gloss

Note

Afro combs or regular wide-toothed combs can be used. Alternatively, make your own. Notches as fine or as coarse as you wish can be cut into a rubber window washer or a cork tile. For smaller jobs like picture frames, cardboard can be substituted, however, it will quickly become soggy.

1 Remove all the knobs and handles from furniture; this allows easier application of the painted finish.

Sand the furniture thoroughly so that the paint will go on smoothly; if the surface is rough, the comb may skim over certain areas and the pattern will not be consistent. Fill any dents or scratches with wood filler before you start.

Apply a base coat of paint with the paintbrush. Lightly sand back when paint is dry. Apply a second coat of paint. Lightly sand when paint is dry. Clean paintbrush in turpentine.

2 Combine acrylic paint with sufficient water to make a thin, watery consistency. Roll the muslin into a ball, dip it into the paint. Using light, even strokes, apply the paint to the furniture. Allow to dry thoroughly.

Apply scumble glaze to furniture with paintbrush; brush strokes should be a little uneven.

3 Drag the combing tool across the wet surface working vertically or horizontally to make a pattern. Wipe any excess paint off the comb with the clean rag; a surplus of paint will cause ridges on the surface.

The scumble glaze is particularly suitable for combing because it doesn't dry quickly, allowing you to change the pattern if you make a mistake. Or you can simply paint on more glaze and start again.

To make a chequered pattern, comb the surface horizontally, then vertically. Unevenly spaced teeth in combs will give a different effect again.

By dragging the comb in wavy lines other patterns can be made too. When the piece of furniture has dried completely, apply a coat of varnish, if desired.

Combing by Georgina Dolling.
Combs: Manfax, enquiries (03) 419 4166. Paints: Porters Original Limewash, enquiries (02) 211 1620. 'Cactus' quilt cover, pillowslips, checked robe: In Residence, Woollahra, NSW; 19th century candlestick: Country Trader, Paddington, NSW.

Stained Glass

Stained glass is one of the oldest architectural crafts; it is difficult to

pinpoint its origins to one time or place. It is basically a manifestation of

the Christian world and may well have been inspired by the art of the

goldsmith and cloisonné enameller. It is the only art which relies com-

pletely on natural daylight for its effect. The panel we have chosen is a

typical leadlight design from the mid to late 1800s. Characteristics of

leadlight of this period were the use of symmetrical, geometric designs

and the predominance of amber glass in the design background.

YOU WILL NEED

Glass off-cuts, for glass-cutting practice

GLASS FOR PROJECT

Pink or mauve 0.3 x 0.3m (numbers 1 to 8 in diagram)

Amber 0.3 x 0.3m sheet (numbers 9 to 16 in diagram)

Green 0.3 x 0.3m sheet (numbers 17 to 24 in diagram)

Red 0.3 x 0.3m sheet (number 25 in diagram)

¼ inch copper foil

Solder: 250g coil 50/50 no resin core

Black patina for solder

Copper wire 1.2mm diameter

Soldering flux (we used Bakers)

Glass cutter (oil-filled recommended)

Soldering iron, at least 80 watts

Grozing pliers, flat-nosed, to snap off pieces of glass

Lead nippers

Straight-edge ruler

Plastic goggles, for eye protection

Small paintbrush

Razor blade

Felt-tip pen

Toothbrush

Rubber gloves

Dishwashing detergent

Sponge

Board for soldering .6m x .6m (particle board or similar)

Shoe polishing brush

Wire or twine, for hanging

NOTE

■ *Most of the materials listed can be purchased from your local leadlight supplier. Most leadlight suppliers will have glass scrap bins, so when buying materials or tools ask for glass scraps with which you can practise.*

■ *Be prepared to spend some time honing your glass-cutting technique on glass scraps.*

■ *Wear safety goggles to protect your eyes from glass fragments.*

■ *As this project uses solder, it is inadvisable for pregnant women to attempt it. If in doubt, contact your GP first.*

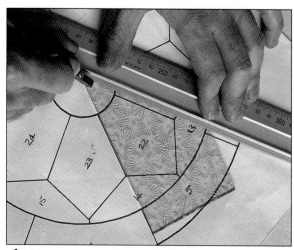

1 **Cutting the glass:** Enlarge diagram by at least 30 percent (best done on a photocopy machine). Number panels according to diagram. Lay glass over the top of the piece of the design you intend to cut. Make use of the straight edges of the glass, they will reduce the number of cuts you have to make. Most cuts for this project are straight ones; this is where your straight-edge ruler is used.

Lay edge of the glass on the inside edge of the line allowing 1mm for adjoining pieces of glass. Position straight-edge ruler over the glass, lining up the ruler with the wheel of your glass cutter, as a sighter at both top and bottom. When satisfied that the ruler is in the correct position, put on safety goggles and cut the nearest edge of the glass from about 2mm in towards you. Score again in the opposite direction. This gives a well defined groove for cutting. Put your glass cutter in this groove. With an even pressure and the glass cutter in an upright position, cut away from you until you reach the far end of the glass. (Never recut over score line as this will shorten the life of your cutter.)

Repeat the procedure for each piece of glass.

Designed and made by Joseph Losurdo, Balmain Leadlight, NSW; enquiries (02) 555 1289.

Diagram 1.

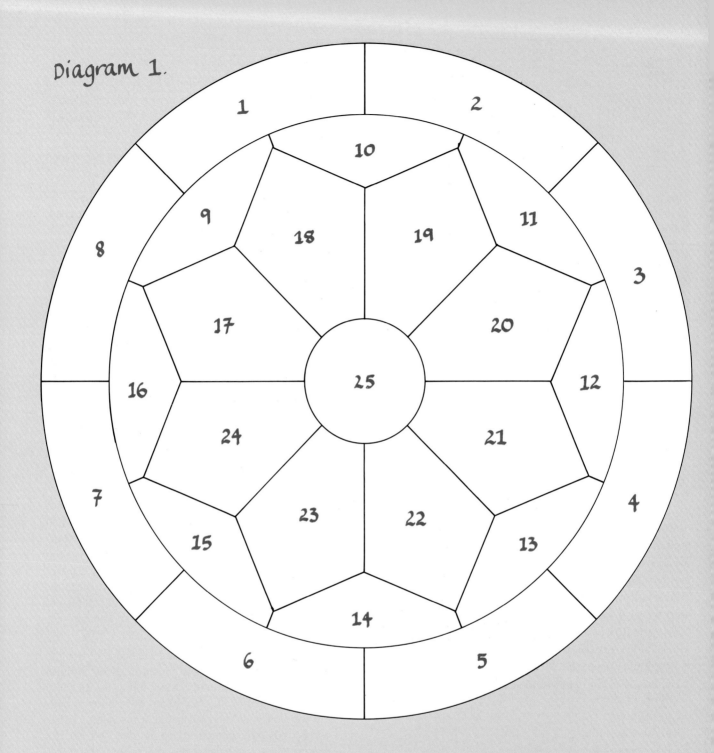

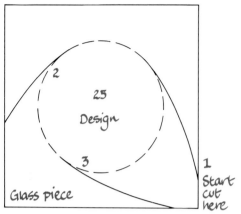

Diagram 2.
Cutting the circle

2 **Breaking the glass:** Place both hands either side of the score line with forearms parallel to the ground and straight out in front of you. (Being in a relaxed, comfortable position makes this procedure easier.)

The score line should be face up; the pressure you exert is downward. Check each cut against diagram. If edges are protruding, grozing pliers can be used to chip them away. Over grozing can lead to the glass breaking, so it may be better to recut the same piece.

3 Grozing pliers are held with front tips parallel to the score line without going over the score line. The pliers can also be used to break narrow pieces too small to be broken by hand. Pliers are held on the piece to be discarded. A downward motion is used, similar to breaking by hand. When you have cut the piece and it fits correctly on top of the design, number it according to the diagram using a felt-tip pen.

Cutting the centre piece: Practise by using offcuts. Cut squarish piece of glass at least 25 percent larger all round than piece No. 25.

Begin cut as normal, following the procedure mentioned in step 1. Make sure your are standing comfortably. Cut slowly, maintaining an even pressure until you reach the opposite edge of the glass. Break away outside edge with grozing pliers. Diagram 2 shows the direction

in which to cut glass. Replace glass on design, making sure that the edge you have cut is in the correct position. Make sure you are in a comfortable position by moving both glass and design so that the next cut is straight out in front of you. Repeat breaking technique and go on with final cut. Chip away over-hanging glass.

Check all pieces as you cut them, as any over size pieces will throw the panel out of shape. Make sure that each of the 25 pieces is the correct size.

Foiling the glass: The method for assembling the glass pieces for soldering begins by attaching copper foil to the edges. The foil comes on a 36m roll; it is adhesive and paper backed.

4 Take a strip of copper foil, peel back paper and attach foil to the glass profile edge. Make sure that the foil evenly overlaps the top and bottom of the piece. Only do this on one side before continuing. Once this is done press foil over edges of glass and rub down with fingers. Overlay the ends of the foil by about 1cm.

Soldering: All soldering must be done in a well-ventilated area. If you are soldering in a small room, have a fan on to blow away fumes. Wear rubber gloves and safety goggles at all times.

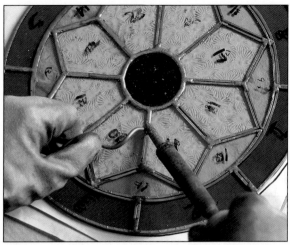

5 Place design on particle board. Put on gloves. Apply liquid soldering flux to copper foil edges with small paintbrush.

Place fluxed central red glass piece on the design. Turn on soldering iron. Take care that soldering iron is sitting in a position where it won't cause any harm. It must be well away from any electrical cords and out of children's reach.

Unwind length of solder, test if solder iron is hot enough by applying solder to tip; if solder melts, the iron is ready.

Place all glass pieces on design. Check they are in their correct position. Carefully tack solder at points at which the pieces of design meet. Once all joints are tacked, start soldering the seams.

With coil ready, position soldering tip just above seam. Apply solder to tip and move along seam until joint is covered. Molten solder takes a few minutes to cool so don't touch the seams while they are cooling. Repeat this process on the back once first side is done. When finished, the seams should be raised about 2mm and have a smooth, rounded appearance.

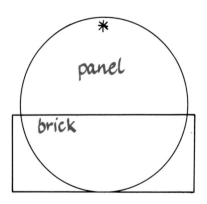

Diagram 3.
Beading the edge.

6 **Beading the edge:** The profile edge of the panel needs to have a thickened uniform layer of solder to keep the foil from being lifted. This is called beading the edge. Beading is done by raising the panel upright, and supporting it with a brick (or reasonably heavy object) on each side, see diagram 3. Take the soldering iron and solder, laying solder on the top edge marked * in the diagram. Gradually move panel as you solder, so that area worked on is always at the top. Switch off iron.

7 **Applying copper rings for hanging:** Bend copper wire at least four times over a rounded pen or pencil to make a closed coil. Use lead nippers to cut two individual rings, bend wire to complete the straightened link. Turn on iron, flux copper rings and cover completely with solder. Hold rings with grozing pliers and solder to position 1, marked in diagram 4. Test for holding capacity. When satisfied move panel so that position 2 is at the top; solder. Switch off iron; it will take at least 10 minutes to cool.

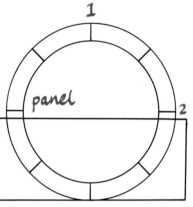

Diagram 4.
Attaching hanging rings

8 **Washing and painting:** Wear rubber gloves. Using a sponge, washing-up detergent and warm water, thoroughly clean your panel. This should be done in a plastic bowl/bucket because flux and patina residues may tarnish your stainless steel sink. Rinse off soap in clean, warm water.

Place wet panel on four sheets of newspaper. With a toothbrush, apply black patina to achieve an even, dull black finish to solder seams and rings. Wash panel in warm, soapy water as before. Rinse. Allow to dry on clean sheets of newspaper.

When panel is completely dry, buff up with clean shoe polish brush. Attach wire or twine to ring and hang near window.

Embroidery

Embroidery is one traditional craft that needs very little equipment.

Here we have featured two different needlework examples. First is a

colourful growth chart, decorated with pixies and woodland creatures.

Each figure is outlined, then worked in satin stitch — useful for filling

areas. For best results, follow each shape accurately and work the

stitches evenly and closely together in the same direction. Our second

piece features a pretty, embroidered country garden scene, worked in a

variety of stitches. Both projects make use of a small embroidery hoop.

Growth Chart

1 To prevent fabric from fraying, oversew on sewing machine, stitching all around edges.

2 **Tracing design:** To transfer the design from pattern to light-coloured fabric, tape design to a sunlit window or a light box and tape fabric in position so that grain line matches the vertical line of the design. Lightly trace design with a dressmaker's pencil. Alternatively, for dark fabrics, place dressmaker's carbon paper face down on right side of fabric. Place design face up on paper. Trace over design using a ballpoint pen or dressmaker's tracing wheel. We placed our figures about 6cm apart, the measuring line about 4cm from the figures and the numbers 10 cm apart.

YOU WILL NEED

90cm x 33cm firmly woven fabric (we used linen)
Dressmaker's pencil
Six-stranded embroidery thread DMC Article
    117 (see illustration for colours)
No.9 crewel needle
Embroidery hoop
Sewing thread
Two x 12cm pieces of wooden dowel
50cm x 3cm-wide ribbon

Finished size: 73cm x 25cm

3 **Sewing the design:** Commence and finish all stitches with a small backstitch within the design area. Work motifs in colours indicated on illustration. Start by placing the fabric in a small embroidery hoop. This keeps the fabric taut. Then, working the vertical measuring line in backstitch, use one strand of thread. The numbers are worked horizontally in satin stitch using three strands.

Use two strands of thread to satin stitch the characters, animals, rocks and mushroom as illustrated below.

NOTE

Embroidery pattern is actual size; enlarge or reduce as desired. Follow stitch colours from design on pages 32 and 33.

Designed by Sue Ninham. Sewing by Jennifer Newman and Rosa Alonso.

Long and short stitch the mushroom cap. Fine details, like the facial features, stars, leaves and the frog outlines are embroidered using straight and backstitches with one strand of the appropriate colour. The spots on the mushroom are French knots using a mixture of two and three strands. These are embroidered over the top of the satin stitch, as are the facial features and some of the rock markings.

The satin stitch is worked on a slight angle. Place the first stitch in the centre of the motif and work towards one side of the motif. Come back to the centre and work towards the other side. This results in an even placement of stitches. Ensure your pencilled design outline is completely covered by the stitches. Place stitches so no fabric shows through and threads are not crowded. Threads should lie flat on the surface when the hoop is removed.

4 **To make up:** Machine stitch a 3cm hem on both edges of chart. Machine stitch a 3cm hem (or wider depending on the size of the dowel) at top and bottom of chart. Press, embroidered side down, on a padded surface. Insert dowel. To hang growth chart, tie ribbon to either side of dowel or sew ribbon to centre back.

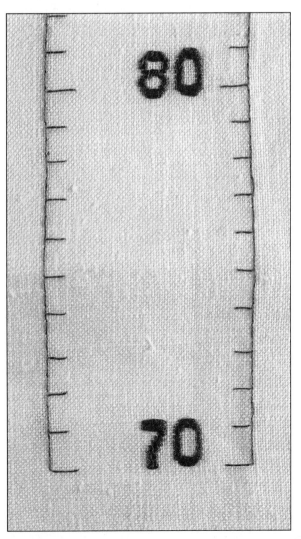

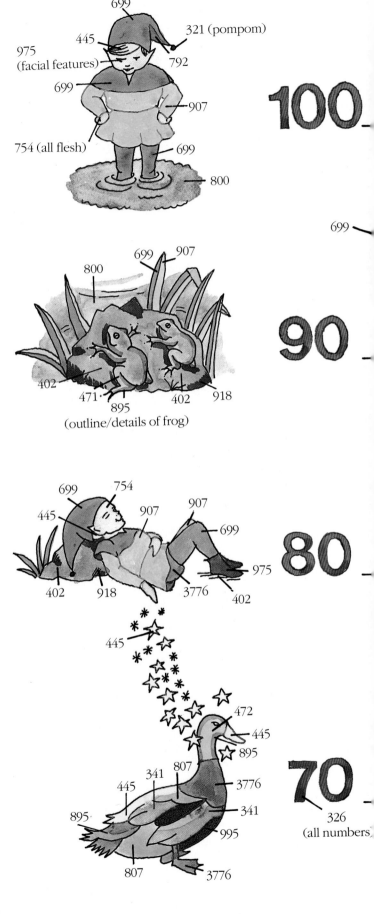

(outline/details of frog)

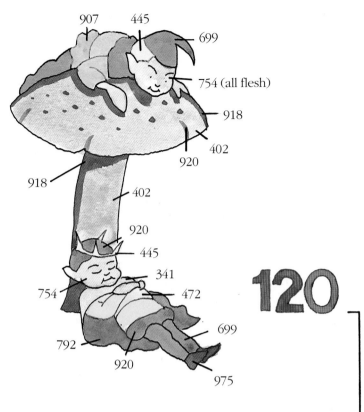

907
445
699
754 (all flesh)
918
402
920
918
402
920
445
341
754
472
699
792
920
975

120

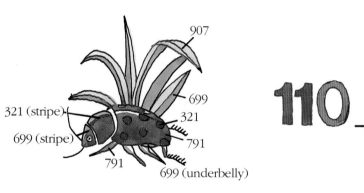

907
699
321 (stripe)
321
699 (stripe)
791
791
699 (underbelly)

110

Garden Picture

YOU WILL NEED

32cm x 22cm fine linen fabric

Six-stranded embroidery threads, DMC Article 117 (see steps for colours used)

Size 10 crewel needle, for all stitches except bullion

Size 8 straw needle, for bullion stitches

Small embroidery hoop

Water-soluble marking pen

Frame for hanging, optional

NOTE

■ *Draw design freehand or trace it onto the fabric with a water-soluble pen.*

■ *Start bottom of gate and rock wall a third of the way up from the bottom edge of the linen. This can be done by ruling a line with a water-soluble felt pen or, very effectively, by folding and finger-pressing the linen.*

■ *Work gate and rock wall, then the pergola and the climbing rose. Follow with the foxgloves, hollyhocks and delphiniums, then the lavender and, finally, the forget-me-nots. A sense of perspective will be achieved by working the background first and then working forward.*

■ *It is important not to carry the thread across the back of the fabric from one flower to the next. The thread will appear as a shadow on the front, especially when white paper is applied to the back in the framing process. Avoid this problem by threading through the stitches of previously worked areas, at the back. All French knots and bullion stitches are worked using a small embroidery hoop.*

1 Pergola and gate: 890, two strands, stem stitch. This provides part of the background.

2 Rock wall: 840 and 842, one strand each, stem stitch. This provides part of the background.

3 Climbing rose: Climbs pergola. Work from base of flowers to tips.

Stems: 319, two strands, stem stitch.

Leaves: 3051, two strands, lazy daisy stitch. Five leaves on different stems.

Roses, centre: 223, two strands, one bullion stitch. Work five twists.

Roses, outer petals: 224 and 225, one strand each, four bullion stitches. Work six twists.

4 Hollyhocks: These are the round, tall flowers on left of gate. Lower flowers have three central French knots; often, flowers have only one French knot. Single French knots represent the buds at the tip of the flowers, see photograph on facing page for details.

Stems: 3363, two strands, stem stitch.

Leaves: 3363, two strands, satin leaf stitch.

Flowers: 224, two strands, buttonhole stitch.

Centres: 223, two strands, French knots.

5 Delphiniums: These are the tall flowers on right of gate.

Stem: 319, two strands, stem stitch.

Leaves: 319, two strands, five lazy daisy stitches.

Flower 1: 792, two strands; 793, one strand.

Flower 2: 793, two strands; 794, one strand.

Flower 3: 794 two strands; 819, one strand.

Use a hoop to work the flowers. Use the three strands together and work French knots, building up the flower until half-way up; then change to one strand of each colour to the tip.

6 Foxgloves: These are the bell-like flowers on either side of gate. (See detail at right).

Stem and leaves: 3346, two strands, stem stitch.

Flower 1: 224, one strand; 225, one strand.

Work the bell-like flowers in buttonhole stitch, making the stitches progressively smaller towards the flower tip.

Flower centre: 3778, two strands, group of French knots.

Flower 2: 3779, one strand; 3770, one strand.

Flower centre: 223, two strands, group of French knots.

Flower 3: 3773, one strand; 3770, one strand.

Flower centre: 3778, two strands, group of French knots.

Blanket stitch

Buttonhole stitch

Stem stitch

Daisy or detached chain stitch

French knots

Bullion stitch

Satin leaf stitch

Straight stitch

Fly stitch

7 Lavender: These are in foreground of scene.
Stems and leaves: 3053, two strands, fly stitch. Add straight stitch for flower stem at the top of fly stitches.

Flowers: 3053, one strand; 3041, three strands; 208, three strands.

Work flowers in bullion stitch, using a size 8 straw needle. Work six or seven twist bullions as in step 3.

8 Forget-me-nots: These are on outside edges of wall.
Stems and leaves: 319, two strands. Work stems in stem stitch, and leaves in grouped lazy daisies.

Flowers: 799, two strands, five French knots around a central French knot in 727.

Designed and made by Jane Matley.

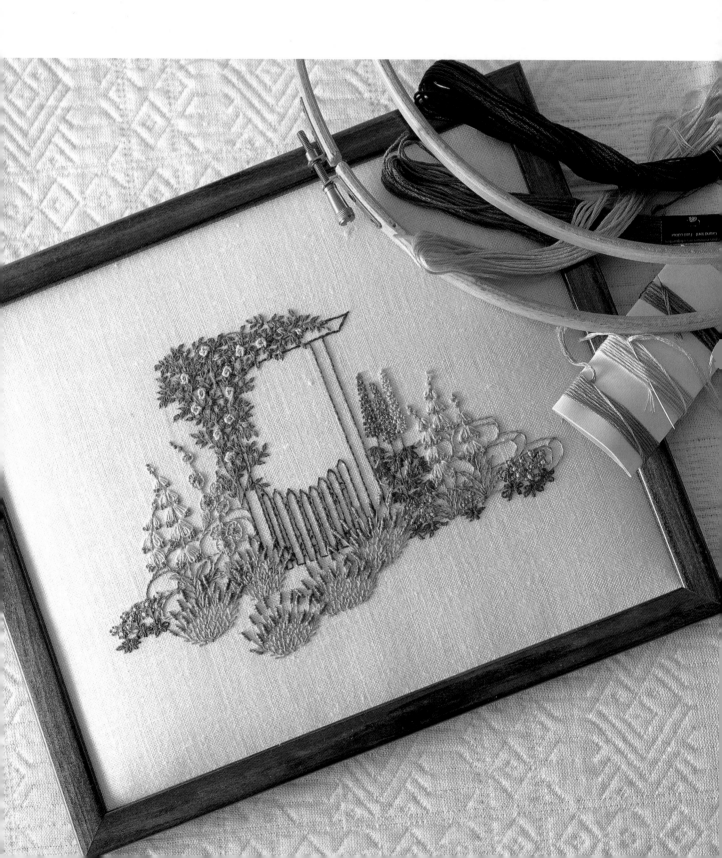

Straight stitch

Fly Stitch

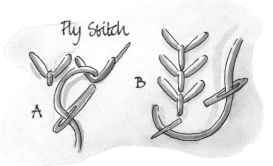

Daisy Stitch or Detached Chain Stitch

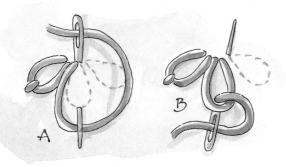

Blanket-stitch & Buttonhole Stitch

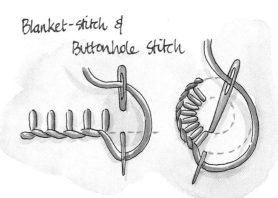

French knots

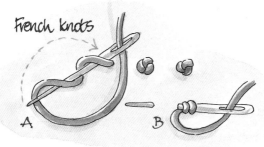

Bullion stitch

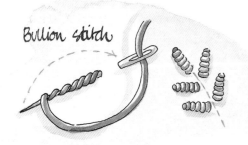

Satin leaf Stitch

Stem Stitch

37

Folk Art

Throughout the ages, people of different cultures have used some form of

painting to decorate their homes. Household furniture, walls, pottery

and floors were adorned with flowers, patterns, animals and even people.

The German word for folk art, Bauernmalerai, literally means farmer

painting. This gives a very clear indication of its humble beginnings; this

was not the work of formally trained artists but that of ordinary folk. Our

antique-finished tray, with its carefully painted, colourful poppies,

leaves and daisies, is not meant for a folk art beginner.

You Will Need

Sandpaper (wet and dry No. 600)

Acrylic paints: (we used Jo Sonja's carbon black, titanium white, napthol red light, Turner's yellow)

Sealer (we used Jo Sonja's sealer)

Tracing paper

Stylus (an empty ballpoint pen or sharp pencil will do)

Dressmaker's chalk pencil

Saral (chalk) paper in a light colour

Eraser

Adhesive tape

Ruler

Paint palate (a white plate or tile will do)

Paint brushes (round: Raphael Series 8480 size 2 or 3; liner: Raphael size 4; flat: 2.5cm)

Varnish (we used Jo Sonja's polyurethane varnish)

FOR ANTIQUE FINISH

Rubber gloves

Lint free rag

Danish oil (we used Cabot's oil, available from hardware stores)

Burnt umber oil paint (we used Windsor and Newton)

Varnish (we used Feast Watson Satin)

Cotton buds

Wax (we used furniture wax)

Made by Anne Colligan, enquiries (02) 451 3004. China from Wedgwood.

Preparing the tray: Sand all rough edges, especially the handles of the tray.

Mix black paint with sealer, (one part paint to one part sealer). Apply one coat to cover tray completely. Allow to dry, apply a second coat. Allow to dry thoroughly.

Sand tray again. Mix a small amount of black paint with red paint. Paint on top of the tray edge and inside handles to highlight them. Allow to dry.

Trace the centrepiece pattern onto tracing paper with pencil. Centre tracing onto tray, secure in place with sticky tape.

Slip light coloured saral paper under tracing. Using a stylus, trace design onto tray.

1 Using chalk pencil, draw a border 1.5cm in from edges of tray. Trace corner pattern onto tracing paper. Place the corner pattern inside the border, secure with adhesive tape. Slip saral paper under tracing. Using a stylus trace design onto it. Repeat design in each corner.

Painting techniques: Squeeze a small amount of paint onto palette. Wet brush with water. Roll brush onto paper towel to remove excess water. Gently pat brush into paint until all fibres are covered.

2 **To paint leaves:** Mix yellow and black paint together to make a gold colour.

Add a little more black to make olive green. Mix two colours: gold and green. Fill brush with green paint, then wipe the loaded brush through the gold on one side only. This is called 'side loading'. Leaf veins are painted using a liner brush loaded with thinner paint (add more water to the paint to give it a thinner consistency).

3 **To paint daisies:** Using a full load of white paint on a round brush, place two strokes close to each other for each petal. Finally, paint centres with random yellow, red and white dots.

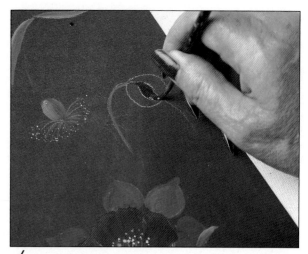

4 **To paint poppy buds:** Vary the colour of buds as illustrated, using red and yellow. Paint centres with an 'S' stroke. When centres are dry complete buds with a green 'C' stroke on each side.

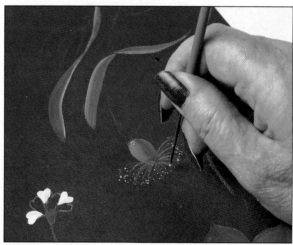

5 Stems and daisy calyxes are painted in thin lines with a liner brush and green paint.

Poppy seed pods: These are the old pods from which all the petals have fallen, leaving only the middle or seed pod.

Paint the base green with 'C' strokes. Shade one side with black and highlight the other side gold. Using liner brush and thinned gold and olive paint, paint stamens with thin lines. Tip stamens with tiny dots of yellow, gold and white.

6 **To paint yellow poppy:** Load a round brush with a thinnish red/yellow mix. Spread this loaded brush on palette into a fan shape. Paint inside top back petal, be careful to follow the shape of the petal. Rinse brush, then pick up a thick load of yellow on tip of brush. Place this thick yellow in a line just below rim of petal. Spread brush into fan shape and push up fanned-out tips of brush into wet yellow paint then drag brush down over previously base-coated petal. Be careful to pull stroke into the curve of the petal – not straight down. Study our illustration for guidance.

Paint the second back petal in the same way *before* painting seed pod and stamens in the centre of flower. The two front petals are painted last.

8 **To paint white poppy:** Brush mix yellow, red and white to desired colour. Place strokes as in yellow poppy back petal. Place white along rim of petal. To achieve turned petal effect, pull the white back from the edge on that part of the petal.

To paint border: Using a liner brush filled with gold and red mix, paint lines along borders. The corner pattern is painted with comma strokes using a gold/red mix. Hold the brush at a 45° degree angle. Steady your hand by placing your little finger on the painting surface. Touch the brush onto painting surface, then pull towards you, gently lifting the brush until it is held upright and only the tip is touching the surface. Slowly lift the brush off the surface. Three 'sit downs' complete the corner. These are oval-shaped dots which are made by sitting the tip of the loaded brush onto the surface of the tray.

Finishing: When all paint is completely dry, rub out any visible chalk marks. Apply one coat of water-based varnish. When dry, put on rubber gloves and rub Danish oil over tray with a disposable cotton kitchen cloth or a lint free rag. Sqeeze out about 1cm burnt umber oil paint and rub this over surface with a lint free rag. Rub off as much oil paint as necessary to give a pleasing colour. After a few minutes take a clean cotton bud and carefully rub back highlights. This is done by rubbing the oil paint off where highlights are required.

Varnishing: Leave tray to dry for a few days, then apply two or three coats of varnish. When dry apply wax and buff for a beautiful finish.

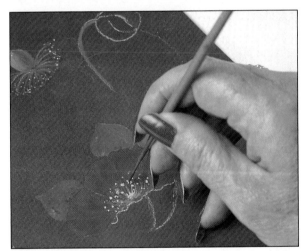

7 **To paint red poppy:** Place a thick rim of red paint below pattern line. Fan out brush, push up and pull down as before, fading out red paint toward centre of flower. When back petals have been painted, paint seed pod as before, then complete with front petal.

Hat Box

Hat boxes have been used for many centuries. In the Edwardian

era, when huge decorated hats were in vogue, hat boxes were at

their peak. Inside was a mound of horsehair or wire gauze which

kept the hat in shape. The earliest boxes were made of painted wood,

some were metal, but these were gradually replaced with sturdy

cardboard covered with printed paper or fabric and lined with

newspaper. In Victorian England, bonnet or hat boxes were made

to match the elegantly-patterned luggage of the aristocracy.

You Will Need

Thick pasteboard for lid top and base

Thin pasteboard for box walls and linings

80cm 115cm-wide cotton fabric

80cm 115com-wide cotton fabric, for lining

40 cm 115cm-wide thin wadding

Masking tape

Fabric glue (we used a glue stick, spray glue and
    craft glue — Stainless 450)

Craft knife

Cutting mat, or suitable surface

Measurements

Lid: A: 310mm-diameter circle

Base B: 300mm-diameter circle

Lid liner: C: 306mm-diameter circle

Base liners: D and E: 298mm-diameter circles
    (two in all)

Lid rim and lid rim cover: F: 1020mm x 42mm
    strips (two in all)

Lid rim liner: G: 1020mm x 39mm strip

Base wall: H: 1000mm x 196mm strip

Base wall liner: I: 1000m x 196mm strip

Note

■ *Large areas are more conveniently glued using a glue stick
or spray-glue. For small areas requiring a strong bond (eg lid
rim cover) craft glue is more suitable.*

■ *Use main fabric to cover all outside pieces. Use lining fabric
for inside pieces. If main fabric has a large pattern, cut carefully, considering pattern and motif placement.*

■ *Cut pasteboard accurately using scissors or a craft knife and
cutting mat.*

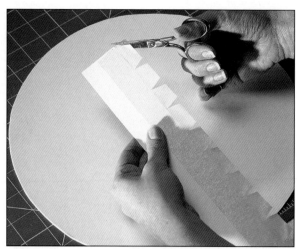

1 **Lid:** Cut A and B from heavy pasteboard to meas-
urements. Cut other pieces from light pasteboard.
Attach a strip of tape along edge of lid rim (F), with half
the width of the tape above rim. Cut V notches from tape.

    Hold F at right angles to the edge of lid (A). Roll rim
(F) around lid (A), adhering tape to the top of A.

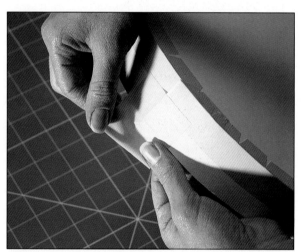

2 Trim ends of F so they overlap by about 10mm. Tape
ends of F together securely.

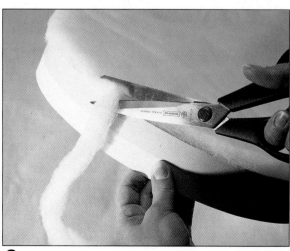

3 Glue a piece of wadding to the flat surface of the lid.
Trim wadding to fit lid.

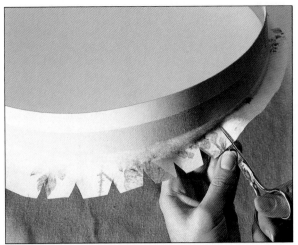

4 Cut a piece of fabric approximately 15mm larger all around than lid. Cut V-shaped notches around edge – they will overlap onto rim. Glue fabric around edges.

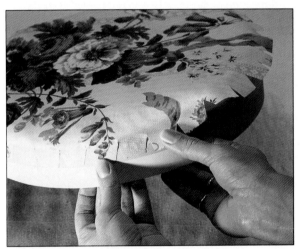

5 Glue notched edges down onto lid rim, pulling fabric taut across the lid.

6 Cut fabric strip 15mm larger than lid rim cover (F). Glue F onto centre of wrong side of fabric. Glue one long edge and one short edge of fabric to other side of F, leaving remaining excess free. Glue covered F around lid rim, placing edge with allowance towards the rim edge.

7 Trim short ends so that the cardboard does not over-lap, but fabric excess overlaps by about 10mm. Glue fabric excess over trimmed end of rim cover. Hold in place until glue bonds.

Turn remaining excess fabric to inside lid rim, glue in place.

Cover lid rim liner (G) with fabric in same way, turn-ing both long edge allowances to wrong side. Fit rim liner (G) inside lid rim, trim one end so that only fabric allowance on one short end overlaps; glue this fabric allowance over the other end.

8 Glue a piece of wadding on one side of lid liner (C); trim to fit. Cut a piece 15mm larger than C. Glue fabric over wadding. Cut notches from fabric allowance; glue allowance on other side of pasteboard.

9 Glue liner in place, inside the lid.

10 **Box:** Cut fabric length 15mm larger than base wall (H). Make base from B and H. Tape wall join.

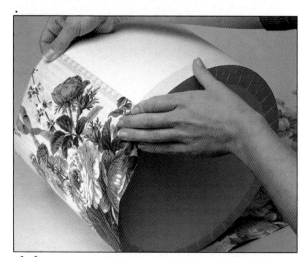

11 Cover wrong side of fabric and outside of box wall with glue. Centre the top and bottom edge of box between top and bottom edges of fabric. Roll the box along fabric making sure box edge is parallel to the fabric edges.

12 Trim fabric across short edge to give 10mm overlap; glue overlap in place. Turn in and glue fabric on top edge of box to inside box. Cut notches from bottom edge of fabric, glue onto box base.

13 Cover box wall lining (I) with fabric, as for lid liner. Fit into box base, trim one end to fit, glue in position. Pad and cover base liner (D) as for lid liner (C), glue inside box base. Cover base liner (E) with fabric only; glue onto the bottom of the box base.

Designed and made by Judy Newman. Tassels: Aviamentos, Newtown, NSW. Photographed at Original Finish, Newtown, NSW.

China Painting

Painted china usually requires firing at high temperatures in a kiln.

Our plate does not require this. But as it is unfired, the finish will not be

food-safe. The colour scheme is inspired by the colours of Medieval

tapestries. It features the fleur-de-lis, Flower de Luce or heraldic lily,

which once symbolised the royal arms of France.

YOU WILL NEED

Large shallow, white-glazed plate (available from kitchenware shops or department stores)

Self-sticking dots (available from newsagents or stationers)

Scissors

Paintbrushes, medium and fine

Mineral turpentine or clear rubbing alcohol

Scalpel

Pencil, hard

Tracing paper

Compass

Carbon paper

Masking tape

Solvent-based ceramic paints in red, yellow, gold, black, green (available from art supply shops)

NOTE

■ *Water-based ceramic paints are unsuitable as they are not available in metallic colours and should not be diluted. Solvent-based paints, however, give the results required, including the delicate colour washes.*

■ *The paints and glazes are NOT food-safe so ensure painted surfaces do not come into contact with the mouth, drink or food. If you want to use an item for food, design it so the contact areas are left unpainted, or have it fired in a kiln. Read the manufacturer's instructions on the paint before you begin.*

■ *Draw a plan before you start of your intended pattern and colour scheme. The elements of the design can be used in a variety of ways so you could decorate each piece individually if you want. A variety of design options is possible: the red plate has a gold fleur-de-lis on the border with circled gold pattern on the main body area. The green version changes the colour and reverses the device pattern. Decorative bowls and coffee cups are a bright and witty addition.*

From the book Designer China *which features a range of hand-painted ceramics decorated with paints that can be set or fixed in an ordinary oven.* Designer China, *by Lesley Harle and Susan Conder, is published by Random House, enquiries (02) 954 9966.*

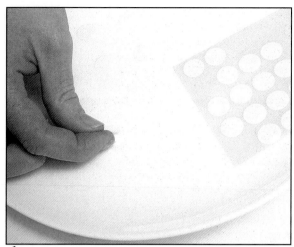

1 Place small, sticky-backed dots randomly over the middle of the plate. Cut some dots in half, and place around the natural edge of the centre, where it meets the rim. Press them down firmly.

2 Paint a small area of the centre thickly with yellow paint. Dip the brush in turpentine or rubbing alcohol and spread the solvent-based ceramic paint, for a colour-washed effect. Work outward to the natural edge. Leave to dry.

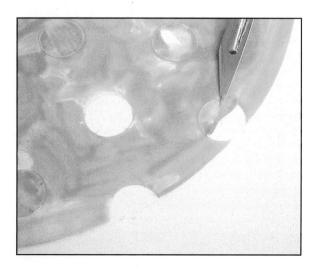

3 Remove the dots, using the edge of a scalpel. If any yellow has bled under the dots, use a fine brush dipped in turpentine or alcohol to remove it.

4 Using the same colour-washing technique, paint the rim red. Paint up to yellow; do not worry if you go slightly over it. Leave to dry.

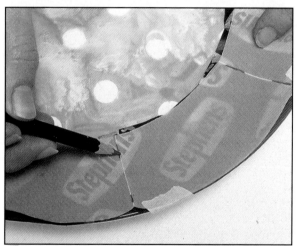

5 Draw around the rim of the plate onto tracing paper. Measure and draw the central circle of the plate onto the paper with a compass. Cut the outer ring of tracing paper out and fold into ⅛ths; these folds mark the points of the tops of the eight fleur-de-lis.

Cut a carbon paper ring the same size, place it, face down, on the plate rim, secure with masking tape. Open the tracing paper out and place it on the rim, secure with masking tape. Using a hard pencil, mark the eight points onto the plate. Remove carbon and tracing paper.

6 Draw a fleur-de-lis, slightly smaller than the depth of the rim, onto a small tracing paper square. Cut a square of carbon paper the same size. Position the motif, aligning the fleur-de-lis point with a mark. Hold in place with your finger. Using a hard pencil, transfer the motif onto the plate. Repeat.

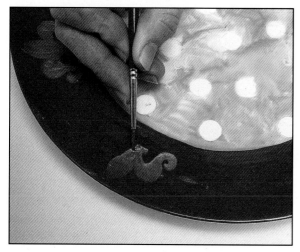

7 Using gold paint, paint the fleur-de-lis motifs, the centres of the white dots, and dots between the fleur-de-lis. Gold ceramic paint is quite translucent, and you may have to paint two coats, especially over the red, to achieve a rich tone. Allow to dry between coats.

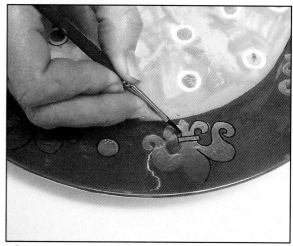

8 Using a fine brush and black paint, outline the motifs and dots. Leave to dry.

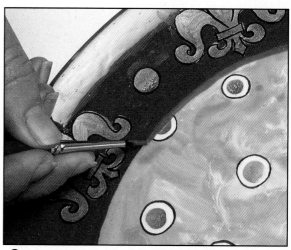

9 Using a medium-sized brush, paint a green line around the edge of the yellow circle. Try to keep the line as even as possible. You may find it easier with a fine brush, going round two or three times. Cover the paint with varnish or glaze.

Rag Rug

There are several traditional ways of making rag rugs. This method is

the braided or plaited rug, which possibly has its origins in the homes of

the early American pioneers where any fabric scrap was considered so

valuable that it was kept and re-used. By carefully choosing colours,

the thrifty, turn-of-the-century housewife could decorate her house

with beautiful home-made rugs. When cheaper floor coverings became

readily available after World War II, rug making went into decline.

With today's interest in recycling, the craft may be making a comeback.

YOU WILL NEED

**Wool fabrics in three different colours, the
amount will vary according to the size of
the rug (we used dark brown, purple
and a pale rose)**

Scissors

Thread

Darning needle

Safety pin or thick rubber band

Finished size: 68cm x 50cm

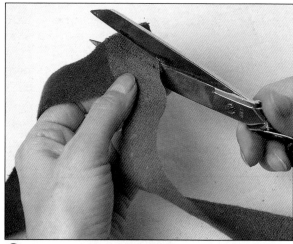

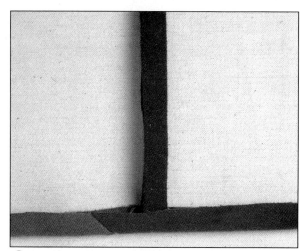

2 Stitch the strips together along the bias, and trim
seam. (This is the way to join all your fabric strips;
the bias seam achieves a smoother, less bulky join.)

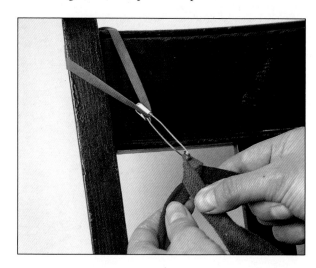

3 Pull the joined strips out flat and fold them in half.
Take the third coloured strip, fold it in half and join
it at right angles to the other two, placing it inside their
fold, forming a T. If you like, you can stitch the three
strands together to keep them in place.

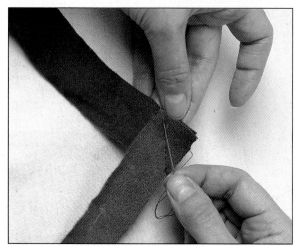

1 Choose good quality wool fabric, two dark shades
and one lighter. Cut wool along grain of the fabric
into strips 3cm wide. Make sure that the strips are of
unequal length – you will then be joining new material
to the strands of braid at irregular intervals, so that the
seam joinings fall at different places in the rug.

Join two of the colours together by placing the strips
at right angles to each other with the right sides of the
fabric facing in.

4 Anchor the strips. One easy method is to attach them with a safety pin and rubber band to a heavy, secure object, such as a chair. Begin braiding by laying the right-hand strip over the centre strip, then the left-hand strip over the centre strip; continue right over centre, left over centre.

5 As you braid, keep folding in the raw edges of each of the fabric strips. Be careful not to twist the strands or you will develop creases which are unattractive (they also catch dirt). Keep the braid tight by pulling the strands sharply *sideways* rather than *down* as you work.

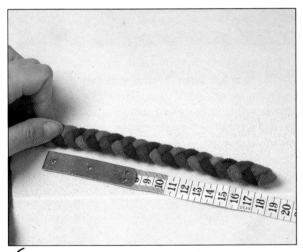

6 The length of the centre braid of an oval rug is determined by the size of the rug you want to make. By subtracting the width of the rug from the length you can work out the length of your centre braid. The rug illustrated here is 68cm x 50cm; therefore, the centre braid should be 18cm long.

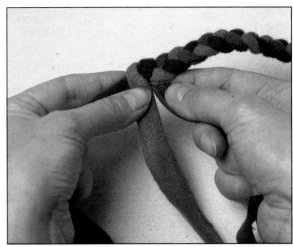

7 The centre of an oval rug is really one long braid bent back to form two parallel braids. To get these to lie flat you can build 'corners' into your braid. For this rug, when the centre braid is 18cm long you can start your corner. This is done by altering your braiding sequence; instead of left over centre, right over centre, work *left over centre*, *left over centre*, then *right over centre* tightly; repeat this sequence once more.

8 You now have your first corner. Continue braiding in the normal sequence.

After you have a fairly good length of braid you will want to begin lacing the rug together. First, secure the braid with a safety pin to keep it from unravelling. When you lace, always lay the braids flat on the table so you can determine whether the rug is being laced properly.

The arrowhead is produced by combining *one* dark shade with *two* light colours; In our rug, the purple was combined with two strands of pale rose. When this row is laced against the butterfly pattern, it produces the arrowhead.

For accenting, we made two rows of braid in wool of darker tones halfway through the rug and then again around the border (two strips in purple and one in dark brown).

Always change colour at the upper curve of the rug, rather than on the straight side.

When the rug reaches the desired size, taper each strip into a long, thin point that extends for about 10 to 15 cm. Cut each strip to a slightly different length so they do not end in the same place.

9 Use a heavy carpet thread or, even better, a thin strand of one of the fabrics which you are using for the braiding as your lacing thread. (If it is a fabric strand make sure it is strong by cutting on the grain of the fabric.) Make a small knot in the strand and thread it onto the longest, thinnest needle you have.

Position the braids so that the loops are not exactly side by side but slightly at an angle to each other. Work the needle through the fold of an inside loop; the knot will be hidden in the fold.

Commence lacing by going under the inside loop of the braid opposite with the needle and bringing it up and out. The needle should *never* penetrate the material. Work back and forth from one braid to another, drawing the thread very tightly so that it is not visible between the loops.

The secret of a flat rug is in the lacing. Each new row of the rug is larger than the previous one – anywhere from 8 to 12 cm. To accommodate the additional length of braid, you skip some loops on the outside braid when lacing. If this is not done, the rug will buckle.

Always skip on the curve of the rug (if done on the straight sides the rug will ripple). Your oval rug has two curves on the top and two on the bottom. Balance the skips on all four curves to keep your rug uniform and symmetrical.

An easy way to decide which loop to skip is to look at the loops just after you have pulled the lacing thread out of a loop on the rug. If the next loop on the braid still to be laced is ahead of the thread, lace it; if the loop is behind the thread, skip it. Skipping a loop is always done on the outside braid, never on the rug itself. Remember that you are trying to ease in the longer outside braid to the shorter perimeter of the body of the rug.

By braiding together two strips in dark tones with one strip in a light tone you will produce a 'butterfly' design as seen on the centre of the rug pictured. This can be curved to produce the classic 'arrowhead' design that is seen surrounding the butterfly pattern.

10 Continue braiding and lacing as far as you can. To finish, insert the strip ends into adjacent loops of the braid with your needle. If the strip end and loop are the same fabric, the end will be less visible. For greater security you may like to stitch the strip ends to the loops with a piece of thread in a matching colour.

Made by Beth Hatton.

Patchwork

Originally, patchwork was a means of extending the life of clothes or rugs: worn or damaged fabric was patched with other leftover material.

Sometimes too, scraps of fabric were joined to make larger pieces, creating a patchwork effect. This is the most common patchwork. Log cabin work, as in our cushion, is another style. It's done by repeating fabric panels, which are made up into a series of square frames, and stitched onto a background. The frames are built up from a central square. The different colours and fabrics within the frames ensures a superb effect.

You Will Need

Small amounts of six different fabrics (use
   photograph as a guide to colours)
40cm x 35cm backing fabric
40cm x 35cm lining fabric
40cm x 35cm polyester wadding
Plastic or cardboard for templates
Quilting thread
Quilting needle
Six stranded thread, DMC Article 117, in colours
   of your choice, optional
Polyester fibre filling

Finished size: approximately 29cm x 27cm

Made by Sylvia Kennedy.

1 Cut templates from patterns over page for pieces 1 to 5. Place templates on wrong side of fabric, using photograph as a guide to fabric colours. Draw around shapes using a pencil; this is the stitching line.

Cut out pieces. Before cutting out each shape, add 5mm seam allowance.

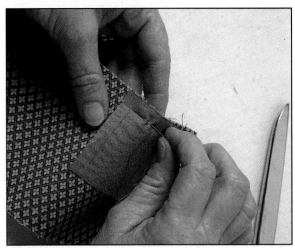

2 **Patchwork:** Following placement diagram over page, join pieces by stitching right sides together in the following sequence. Open out piece 2 (roof), place piece 1 (chimney), 3cm from right-hand side of piece 2. Stitch, open out and press flat.

3 Stitch three x piece 4 together, then a piece 5 at one end, followed by three x piece 4. This forms the top storey of the house. Stitch this section to longer edge of piece 2, centred, as shown.

5 **Embroidery** (optional): For all embroidery use six strands of thread and colours of your choice. Work window panes in single stitch in each direction; work a stitch where threads intersect, to hold them in place.

Work flower pots with a row of vertical straight stitches, weaving horizontal stitches over and under vertical threads to form a basket weave pattern.

Work flower stems in straight stitch and stitch flowers in French knots.

Work door knob in satin stitch.

Quilting: Place patchwork and lining wrong sides together, with wadding sandwiched between. Using quilting needle and thread, take small running stitches to quilt patchwork cushion as desired. (For emphasis, we outlined the roof and doors.)

To make up: Place quilted top and backing fabric right sides together. Stitch together, leaving small opening along one edge. Clip corners, turn right side out.

Fill with polyester fibre, stitch opening closed.

4 Open out and stitch a piece 3 to raw edge of top storey section. Join remaining 4 and 5 pieces to form lower storey of house. Join to raw edge of piece 3, and finish with remaining piece 3 at bottom edge of house.

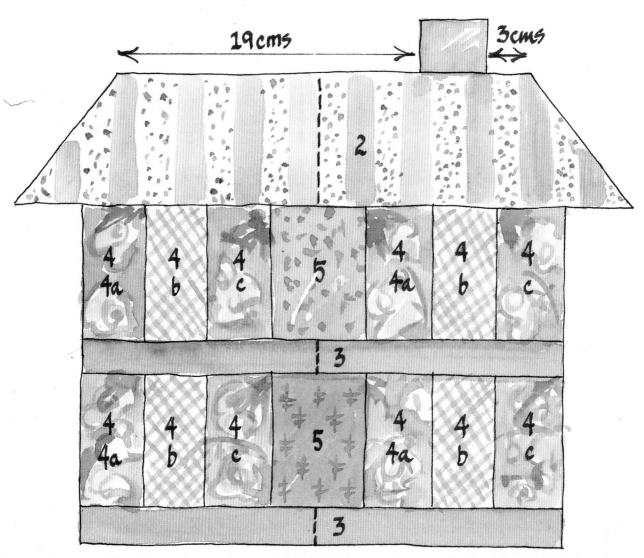

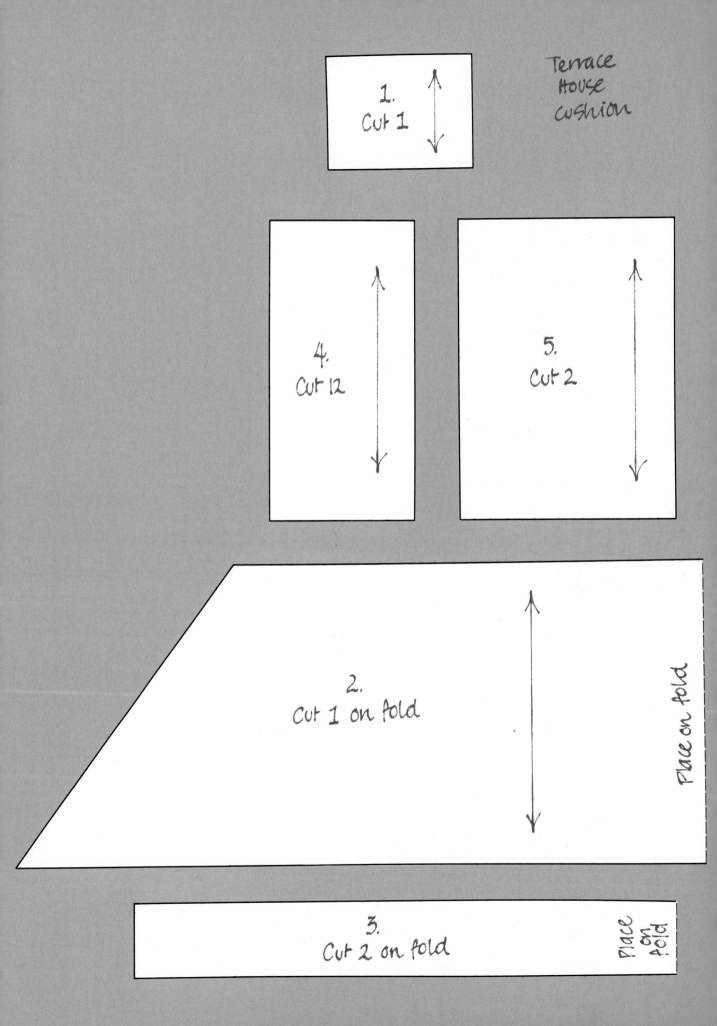

Terrace
House
cushion

1.
Cut 1

4.
Cut 12

5.
Cut 2

2.
Cut 1 on fold

Place on fold

3.
Cut 2 on fold

Place on fold

Gilding

Gilding has long been used to enrich architecture, paintings,

manuscripts, furniture and frames. Gold leaf, (gold that has been ham-

mered into filmy, thin sheets), enchanted Byzantine and Baroque

artists who used it lavishly in their works of art. The Egyptians adorned

mirror frames with it; while the European aristocracy of the 17th

century filled their homes with paintings set in ornate, gilded frames.

The origins of our picture frames stem from early Christian altar paint-

ings and artefacts, where gold leaf was applied to halos and costumes.

YOU WILL NEED

Timber frame for gilding

Timber putty

Fine sandpaper

Acrylic paint primer (we used Artists' Acrylic Gesso Primer)

Poster paint (we used reddish brown Pelikan Plaka)

Shellac

Gold size (we used Windsor and Newton Japan Gold Size)

Gold leaf, in the form of transfer gold which is interleaved with tissue paper (available from art supply stores)

Assorted brushes

Cotton wool

NOTE

■ *The method we have used here is known as oil gilding. It uses transfer gold which has a thin, waxy coating which adheres to tissue paper, making handling of the delicate gold leaf much easier. It is more durable than water gilding.*

■ *Traditionally, oil gilding requires the use of gesso and bole, but for convenience, these easily can be substituted with acrylic primer paint and poster paint respectively.*

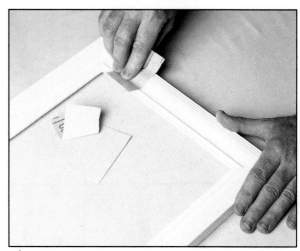

1 Fill any holes in frame with timber putty, sand smooth. Paint with acrylic primer, allow to dry. Sand until smooth.

2 Paint frame with two or three coats of poster paint, allow to dry. The paint gives the colour which will show through the gold, traditionally a warm reddish brown is used.

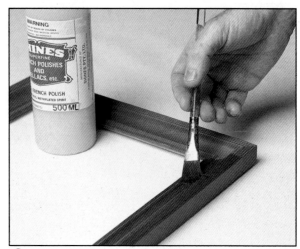

3 When poster paint is completely dry, seal the frame with a coat of shellac, allow to dry.

4 Apply gold size to area on frame to be gilded. It is usual to leave the sides of a frame ungilded.

5 Set frame aside for about 15 minutes, or until size is drying but still slightly sticky.

Applying gold: Lay a sheet of transfer gold onto frame, gold side down (the gold will adhere to the size). Through the tissue paper, very gently smooth the gold into the crevices of the frame using your fingertip.

6 Lift off the sheet of tissue, then reapply over any areas which are not covered with the gold (only those areas where size is still showing, will take up gold). Repeat until desired area is covered with gold. Allow several days for the size to harden.

7 When frame is completely dry, using a piece of cotton wool, gently smooth down the gold leaf to give a shiny polished finish.

The plaster pieces pictured above were painted and gilded in the same way as the frame.

Frame gilding by Ken Hobson. Plaster gilding by Dawn Hobson. Books: La Maison du Livre, Balmain; tassel: Aviamentos. Photographed at Original Finish, Newtown, NSW.

Applique

From the French, appliquer, meaning to apply, applique is the centuries-old needlecraft of attaching pieces of fabric onto a contrasting material background. Examples of this attractive but simple technique can be found all over the world. Applique is often made more elaborate by using the additional skills of quilting and patchwork. Traditionally, it is found on home furnishings like bedspreads. Our two projects feature two types of applique; a traditional hand-sewn picture, decorated with embroidery and quilting, and a machine-worked cushion cover.

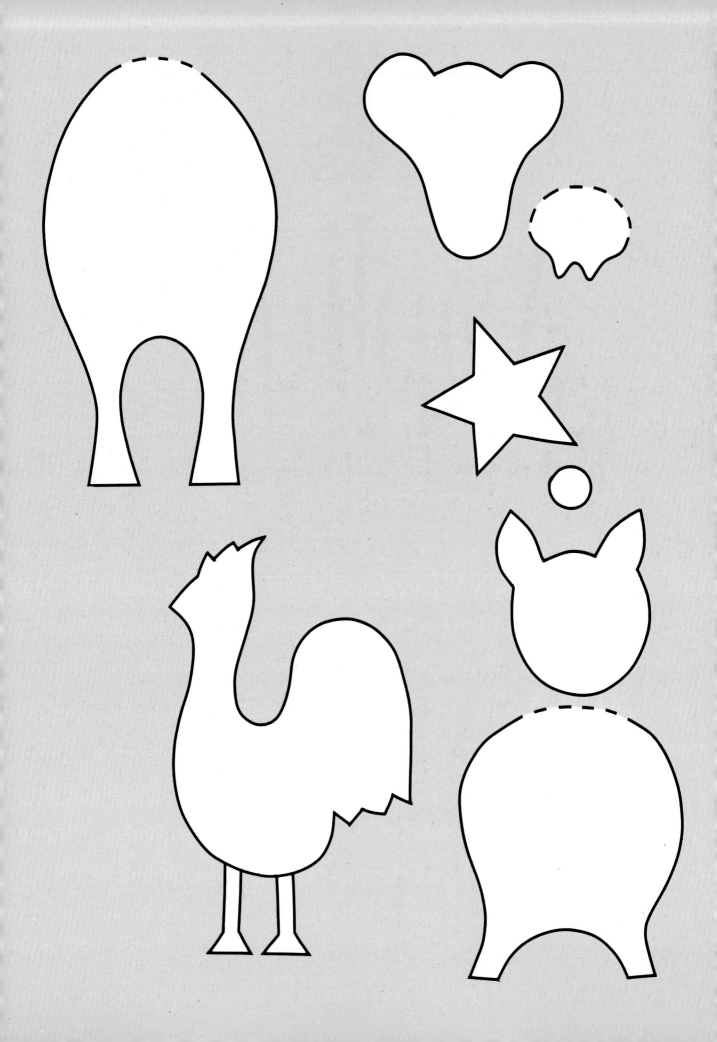

Hand Applique

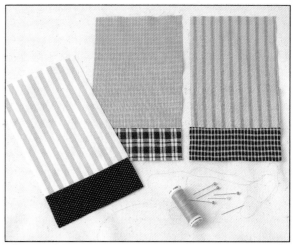

1 Using 1.5cm seam allowance, stitch one large piece dark blue and white fabric to one small piece of light blue and white fabric across one 13.5cm edge. Press seam towards darker fabric. Repeat for remaining pieces to give three pieced rectangles.

2 Trace patterns onto tracing paper, cut out. Place pattern pieces on red fabric prints considering the position of fabric pattern and referring to picture for position of pieces. Cut out, adding 5mm seam allowance around each piece. Note rooster's legs are embroidered, not appliqued.

YOU WILL NEED

Three 20cm x 13.5cm pieces light blue and white fabric

Three 13.5cm x 7cm pieces dark blue and white fabric

Small amount extra dark blue and white fabric, for star

Small amount various red print fabrics

Six stranded embroidery thread, in red and navy

34.5cm x 24cm thin wadding

40cm x 90cm-wide calico fabric

Tracing paper

Scissors

Lead pencil

Sewing thread

Quilting thread

Applique needles, optional

Quilting needle

Finished size: 31.5cm x 21cm

NOTE

■ *Any material scraps can be used for applique, however it is particularly effective if contrasting coloured fabrics are used. Light to medium weight smooth-surfaced fabrics are best to work with. Loosely woven or bulky materials are much harder to use.*

■ *If the finished project, like the cushion cover, will need washing, ensure that fabric choice can be washed.*

Designed and made by Judy Newman. Photographed at Original Finish, Newtown, NSW.

3 Place fabric pieces on blue and white rectangle noting stitching order and overlapping pieces.

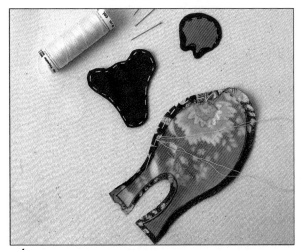

4 Centre paper pattern on wrong side of each fabric piece, pin. Turn seam allowance to wrong side, tack in place through paper. Edges which will be overlapped by another piece need not be turned under (these are indicated by broken lines on pattern). Remove pins.

Pin applique pieces in position on background rectangles, considering order of stitching.

5 Blind stitch around each piece, making sure stitches are almost invisible and using matching thread and applique. See diagram below.

Using sharp lead pencil, draw in rooster's legs, embroider in satin stitch using three strands of red thread. On pig's nose, stitch two French knots, using two strands of navy thread.

Piece (stitch) the three rectangles together along their long edges. Place the completed applique picture on a same size calico piece (wrong sides together), with wadding sandwiched between.

Quilt around each motif using running stitch and quilting needle and thread.

Frame as desired (depending on frame, it may be necessary to stitch a border of calico strips around the finished piece to give extra allowance).

blind stitch

Machine Applique

YOU WILL NEED

40cm x 115-wide calico fabric
38cm square cotton fabric, in pink
38cm square of cotton fabric, in green
Two 38cm squares of fusible webbing
Scissors
Matching threads
Tracing paper
Typing paper
35cm square cushion insert

Finished size: 35cm x 35cm

— — Broken lines represent one quarter of design

↕ straight grain

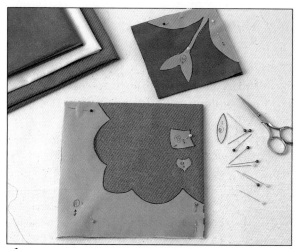

1 Enlarge pattern to 19cm x 19cm. Trace off pattern onto tracing paper, cut out pattern pieces. (Pattern represents one quarter of design.) Mark straight grain with an arrow on each pattern piece. Using a hot iron and following manufacturer's instructions, fuse wrong side of pink and green fabric pieces to webbing.

Fold fabric into quarters, pin main pattern pieces on fabric following straight grain.

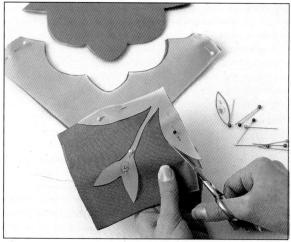

2 Cut around pattern carefully. Cut out small pieces (four small petals, four large buds and eight leaves) from remaining fabric.

3 Open out fabric pieces. Remove backing paper from fused fabrics.

Cut a 38cm square of calico for cushion front.

4 Place main pattern pieces, fusible webbing side down, onto calico. Fuse into position on calico as before. Repeat for smaller petal pieces in centre of design.

Place a piece of typing paper under the calico.

5 Using matching threads and a machine satin stitch (close zigzag), stitch around each applique piece keeping machine speed even and turning fabric evenly as it is stitched.

Remove paper from wrong side. Press.

Cut two 38cm x 26cm calico pieces for back. Stitch a double 1.5cm-wide hem on one long edge of back pieces.

Place one back piece wrong sides together with front, matching raw edges – back pieces will overlap. Stitch around all edges. Trim and neaten seam, turn through. Place cushion insert in cover.

Designed and made by Judy Newman.

Papier Mache

Translated literally, papier mache means chewed paper. Some early

examples of this art include lacquered war helmets and pot lids made in

China around 200AD. The art of papier mache was carried to Europe

via the trade routes and adopted with great enthusiasm. In the 18th and

19th century there were papier mache factories in Europe producing

vast amounts of ornaments and moulds. In the 1790s, an entire church in

Norway was made of papier mache. Boards of papier mache have even

been used as partitions on ocean liners.

Dolls

YOU WILL NEED

Plasticine
PVA glue (we used Aquadhere)
Strips of newspaper
Petroleum jelly (we used Vaseline)
Adhesive tape
Tissue paper
Craft knife
Paints (acrylic or poster)
Darning needle
Hat elastic
Varnish or clear spray gloss

NOTE

■ *Building up layers of papier mache can be time consuming. Each layer must be completely dry before you add the next. It can take a couple of days for each outer layer to dry.*

■ *There are two methods of papier mache: Laminating which involves building up layers of glue-soaked paper; and pulping which involves boiling the paper, pulping it, mixing it with glue and shaping it. Our projects use the laminating method.*

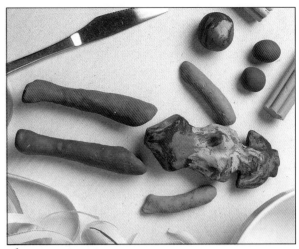

1 Using plasticine, make a simple five-piece shaped mould with your hands. Include the head shape in the central body piece. Ensure that the surface of the plasticine is smooth. Coat the plasticine liberally with petroleum jelly.

2 Using small strips of newspaper soaked for a few minutes in PVA glue and water (one part glue to 10 parts water), cover each plasticine body piece with newspaper strips, overlapping each section until entirely covered. You'll need to use small pieces of newspaper for awkward areas like the feet and neck contours. Allow time to dry.

Continue covering plasticine until you have built up four layers. Allow to dry thoroughly. As the layers build up, drying time will take much longer. The final layers can take a couple of days to dry thoroughly.

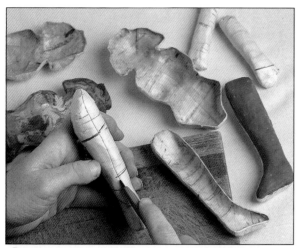

3 Make a clean, straight cut into each section with a sharp knife, carefully remove the newspaper shells from the moulds; discard plasticine.

Rejoin the two empty halves using small pieces of adhesive tape to hold body piece together.

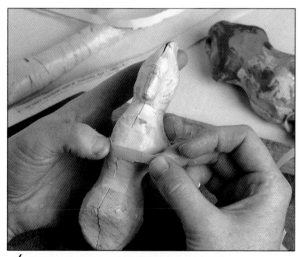

4 Apply another three layers of newspaper to each newspapered limb to cover the joins. Allow to dry. When completely dry, apply a layer of tissue paper as a final coat; this will ensure a smooth finish.

Paint all body pieces with white paint; they may need up to three coats to cover any visible newsprint. Allow to dry between each coat.

Paint doll as desired using acrylic or poster paints. Designs can be as simple or ornate as you like. You could sew clothes to fit the doll.

5 Using a darning needle, carefully pierce holes in arms, legs and central section, as shown in picture, Thread black hat elastic to connect the joints; secure.

6 Coat the doll with a protective layer of varnish or clear spray gloss.

Bowls

You Will Need

Petroleum jelly (we used Vaseline)
Newspaper strips
Sharp scissors
PVA glue
Fibrous paper (we used handmade Japanese wrapping paper)
Acrylic paint (in a colour to highlight paper colour)
Varnish or clear spray gloss

1 Select a bowl, dish or plate of a suitable shape and size to be used as a mould. Liberally coat the inside of the bowl with petroleum jelly; make sure all the surface is well covered.

Tear newspaper into strips about 13cm x 2.5cm long. Soak strips in a mixture of glue and water (one part glue to 4 parts water). Remove when strips are well coated, squeeze out excess water, place strips in overlapping rows on the inside of the greased bowl. Allow layer to dry out completely before placing another layer down.

Repeat above step until seven or eight layers have been built up. Place each alternate layer of newspaper in the opposite direction to the layer underneath. Build up as many layers as necessary to ensure that the papier mache shape is sturdy and has no weak spots. Allow to dry thoroughly. As the layers build up, the drying time can take a couple of days between coats.

Remove newspaper from bowl. Cut off the uneven edges on the rim with sharp scissors. Seal the cut edge with smaller pieces of torn newspaper until the rim is even and smooth and is of the same thickness as the rest of the bowl.

2 Apply a final layer using unprinted newspaper (the outside borders of newspaper pages is best). This will ensure that no newsprint will be visible beneath any lightly coloured overlay of paper. Allow to dry.

Place pieces of fibrous paper into the glue mixture until glue soaks through paper. Carefully place on papier mache bowl, pressing them in place gently as the paper is much softer than newspaper. A combination of colours or textures can be used.

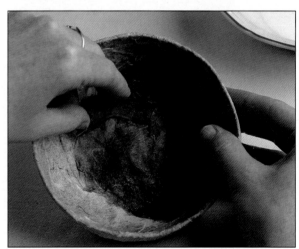

3 For added effect, apply a wash of acrylic paint and water to emphasise the texture of the paper. Start by using only a little colour, if desired, to maintain the subtle hint of colouring. Allow to dry thoroughly.

Following manufacturer's instructions, seal bowl with three coats of protective varnish or clear spray gloss.

Papier mache projects made by Anne Ross-Kasis. Child's antique pram from Broadway Antiques, Glebe, NSW.

Quilting

Believed to be one of the oldest forms of needlework, quilting has been

used throughout the ages on petticoats, bedcovers, waistcoats, cushions,

wall hangings and even armour! Hand-quilted stitches are small and

even and the fabric used should reflect the light so as to show off the

sculptured surface to its best advantage. We opted for a simple shell

design repeated across the face of this satin cushion. A quilting hoop was

used to hold the three layers of material together securely; the hoop can

be easily moved to and from the area on which you intend to work.

YOU WILL NEED

70cm piece of 90cm-wide fabric for front, length includes enough fabric for pleated edge (we used duchess satin)

43cm square cotton lawn fabric (for backing)

43cm square polyester wadding

Tailor's chalk pencil

Cardboard

Scissors

Quilting needle

Quilting thread

Quilting hoop

Thimble

35cm square cushion insert

Press studs

Finished size: 35cm x 35cm (plus frill)

15mm seam allowance is included

NOTE

■ *To start a line of quilting: Knot end of thread, insert needle from top through all three layers. Gently but firmly pull the thread from underneath so that the knot slips through the top layer, and sticks in the filler. Cut off any visible thread on the surface.*

■ *To end a line of quilting: Make a knot on top of quilting surface. Place needle a stitch length away and run needle through filler. Bring needle up, gently pull the thread so that the knot slips through the top layer. Cut off thread end close to the surface.*

1 Trace design onto stiff cardboard to make a template. Cut out template with sharp scissors.

2 Cut a 43cm square of satin fabric for cushion front. Place template on right side of satin fabric. Clearly draw around template with tailor's chalk pencil, beginning in centre and working to within 4cm of the edges. Markings must be sufficiently strong to last through all handling.

Sewing and quilting by Betty Smith.

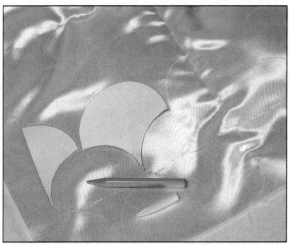

3 Place cushion front and lawn fabric wrong sides together with wadding between. Pin together. Tack layers across centre top to bottom, side to side and around the edges.

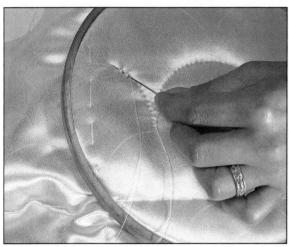

4 **How to quilt:** When quilting by hand, the trick is to use an even running stitch that is short and closely spaced so that it looks like an unbroken line; a length of quilting thread no more than 50cm long is best. Ideally, the stitches should be fine (about 2mm long), and even on both top and backing. Use a hoop for best results.

Beginning around the centre, and working out to one side, take needle between thumb and forefinger, take a few stitches, and push needle through with middle finger. (You can wear a thimble on your middle finger of your working hand.) To be sure needle penetrates all layers, hold other hand beneath the surface so that you can feel the point of the needle each time a stitch is taken.

When quilting is complete, brush or wipe off tailor's chalk with a clean, dry towel.

To make up cushion: Cut three 90cm x 8cm strips of fabric for frill. Stitch short ends together to make a continuous loop. Press in half with wrong sides together to give a 4cm-wide piece.

Trim cushion front to 38cm square. Mark the midway

point along each side of the cushion. Fold frill piece into quarters, mark quarter points with a pin. Pin frill quarter points to midway points on cushion front. Fold frill into pleats, evenly spaced approximately 2cm apart, so frill fits around cushion front, allowing extra fullness at each corner. Tack pleats in place, stitch frill to cushion 1.5cm from raw edges.

Cut a 38 x 20cm and a 38cm x 28.5cm piece for back. Stitch 2cm hems on one 38cm edge of each back piece. Place narrow back piece on cushion front, with right sides and raw edges together, and keeping frill towards centre of cushion.

Place remaining back piece on cushion front overlapping hemmed edges of backs, so backs fit front. Stitch together over previous stitching. Trim and neaten seam, turn right side out.

Sew fasteners to back opening. Insert cushion filler.

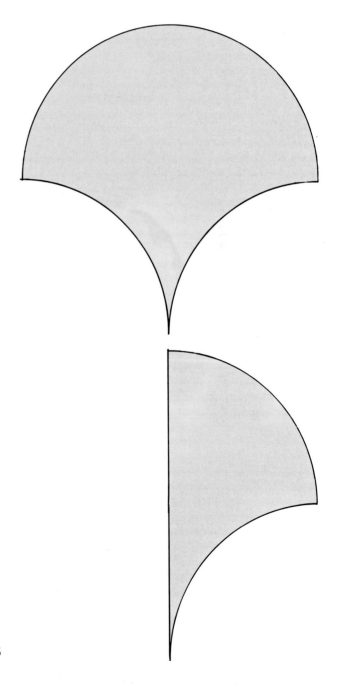

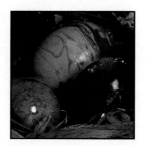

Marbling

Like so many skills, the art of marbling on paper came from the East

via various trade routes, through Turkey during the Crusades. By the

15th century, Venetian craftsmen had discovered how to marble. The

technique became such a highly prized skill in workshops that the secret

process was broken down so individuals only knew particular areas of the

whole method. Even today, Turkish and Venetian marbling is renown

all over the world. We have used a simple method to decorate both eggs

and paper: it can be easily achieved at home with a little practice.

Marbled Eggs

You Will Need

Hen's eggs
Large hat or drawing pin or egg pricker
2 bowls, large and small
Liquid detergent
Clean, absorbent cloth (white if possible)
Cotton gloves, optional
Wooden skewers
Elastic bands
Polystyrene block, for drying eggs
Glass jar
Alum (available from chemist)
Rubber gloves
Wallpaper size (available from hardware shops)
Muslin or gauze
Spoon or ladle
Paintbrushes or eye dropper
Oil-based paints (we used model paints:
    Humbrol, Model Master, Tamiya)
Paper towels
Newspaper
Gold crowns (available from bead suppliers;
    sequins can be used)
Craft glue
Water-based quick-drying varnish

Note

Choose smooth unblemished eggs; indentations, grooves, or watermarks will show through the pattern.

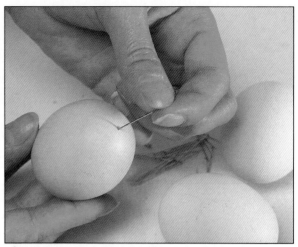

1 **Blowing an egg:** Hold the egg tightly and make a small hole at the top with a pin or egg pricker. Bore a neat, round hole in the shell about 2mm wide. Repeat process at other end of egg.

Hold one end of the egg over the small bowl. Placing your mouth over the hole at the other end, blow out the contents. To make this easier, you can push the pin up into the egg yolk and stir it around a little to make the contents flow more freely.

Fill empty egg with warm water, shake and blow again. Repeat this process until the expelled water is completely clear. Repeat process with all eggs.

2 Gently wash the eggs by hand in a large bowl containing warm water and a little detergent. Do not scratch the surface with your nails or a scourer because the shells will be marked and the protective film which covers them will be removed, making it impossible for the paint to be absorbed evenly.

Dry the eggs carefully with a clean, absorbent cloth. From now on, do not handle the eggs unless you are wearing cotton or clean rubber gloves. Grease from your bare hands will be absorbed on the surface and will repel the paint. Empty bowl, wipe dry.

3 Wind an elastic band onto a skewer, about 2-3cm in from one end. Carefully insert the skewer into the egg so that the egg is resting on the band. Insert the other end of the skewer into the polystyrene block. Repeat with remaining eggs. Leave eggs for a day or so to dry out completely.

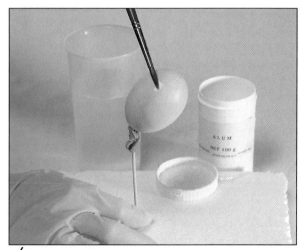

4 Mix 30g of alum to 1 litre of water in a jar. Apply two coats of alum mixture to the eggs, allowing about 5-10 minutes' drying time between coats. The alum helps the paint to adhere to the shells.

5 Put on rubber gloves. Mix up size according to manufacturers' instructions; it should be the consistency of thickened, not whipped, cream.
Strain the size through the muslin to get rid of lumps. Spoon size into large bowl, until bowl is about half-full.

6 Using a paintbrush or eye dropper, drop a few spots of your chosen paint colours onto the surface of the size. You must work quickly because the size will gradually thicken and may form a film on the surface. Don't attempt to use more than one or two colours at first. Each spot of colour should float on the surface and form a little circle.

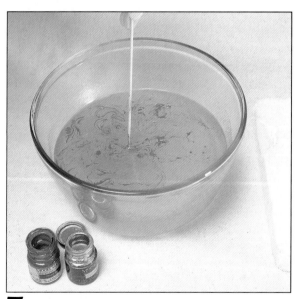

7 Using the pointed end of a skewer or a thick sewing needle pull or swirl the islands of paint into patterns.

8 Insert another skewer into the hole in the other end of the egg. Holding the skewers, steadily lower the egg horizontally until it is totally immersed. (The egg collects the colour as it passes through the design.)

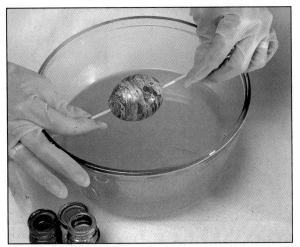

9 Lift out egg quickly, turning it vertically to prevent it from being marbled twice. If the colours start to run, gently blow onto the egg.

10 Push the end of one of the skewers into the polystyrene so the egg dries in an upright position.

11 To remove paint from the mixture between each dipping, lay a piece of paper towel on the surface to soak up the colour; remove and discard. Skim the surface with newspaper strips to remove any remaining colour. The surface should be clear before you add more paint to begin a new pattern for the next egg.

You may have to add more water to the size to return it to the desired consistency before dipping the next egg.

12 Once the eggs are dry, apply at least two coats of varnish, following manufacturers' instructions. Use even brushstrokes, working only in one direction. When dry, glue on the crowns or sequins to cover the holes at either end.

Marbled Paper

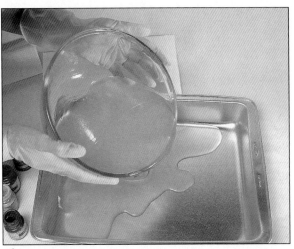

You Will Need

Sheets of paper (we used white, recycled, smooth
   90 gsm stock)
Large deep-sided baking dish
Cold water
Large bowl
Wooden skewers
Glass jar
Rubber gloves
Wallpaper size (available from hardware shops)
Muslin or gauze
Spoon or ladle
Oil-based paints (we used model paints:
   Humbrol, Model Master, Tamiya)
Paper towels
Newspaper
Fork, for mixing in size
Spoon
Mineral turpentine, to clean paintbrushes

1 Put on rubber gloves. Mix up size according to
manufacturers' instructions; it should be the consistency of thickened, not whipped, cream. Strain size through muslin skin to get rid of lumps. Pour enough stained size into large deep-sided baking dish to cover bottom of dish to a depth of approximately 3 cm.

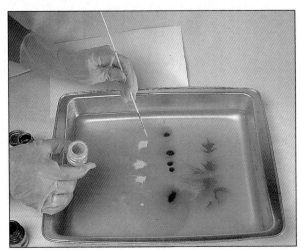

2 Using a skewer, paintbrush or the eye dropper, drop
a few spots of paint of the desired colours onto the surface of the size. (You must work quickly as the size may form a film on the surface if it is too thick.) Each spot of colour should float on the surface and form a little circle. To change patterns between dipping the paper, you can re-swirl the paints.

Note

*Alternatively, you could use carrageen moss instead of
wallpaper size. But it is difficult to work with and is mainly
used by professional marblers. It adds body to the water so it
holds the paint on the surface. It is readily available from good
art supply shops.*

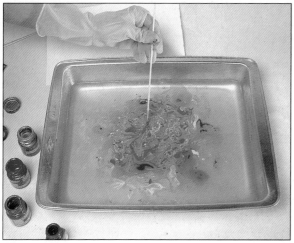

3 Using the pointed end of a skewer or a thick sewing needle pull or swirl the islands of paint into patterns.

4 Take sheet of paper, and at a 45° angle, lower paper gently and quickly onto the surface of the mixture.

5 Remove paper almost immediately from dish, holding one of the corners and lifting out quickly at the same 45° angle.

6 The paper will have collected the coloured patterns on the top of the mixture. Place 'marbled' paper on clean, surface until dry.

7 To clean the mixture of paint between each dipping, lay a piece of paper towel on the surface to soak up paint, remove and discard paper towel. Skim the surface with strips of newspaper to remove any excess. The surface should be clear before you add more paint.

You may have to add more water to the size to get it back to the desired consistency before the next dipping.

Cut paper into various sizes and shapes to make book marks, gift tags, greeting cards or, if you are really ambitious, wrapping paper.

Glass bottles courtesy of Georgina Dolling.

93

Heirloom Sewing

Heirloom sewing is a very delicate and laborious style of handstitching

which uses only natural fabrics such as silk, cotton and linen. And, as

the name suggests, the finished pieces — such as christening robes,

lingerie, fine table linen and our delightful baby's pillow — are designed

to be cherished and passed down from generation to generation.

You Will Need

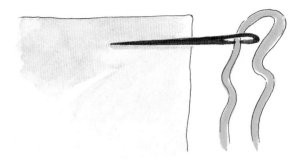

30cm x 90cm-wide cotton voile fabric

50cm x 1cm-wide flat, cotton, insertion lace with entredeux edging

1m pink entredeux

50cm x 1.5cm-wide flat, cotton, single-edge lace with entredeux edging

2.1m x 3cm-wide flat, cotton, single-edge lace

Six stranded thread, DMC Article 117, in pale green, for embroidery

1m x 4mm-wide silk ribbon in two shades of pink, for embroidery

30cm x 90cm-wide cotton lawn fabric, for insert

Polyester fibre filling

Finished size: 28cm x 20cm

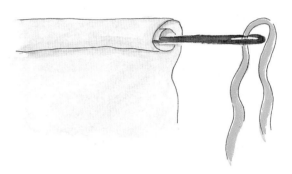

Note

■ *This pillowcase uses traditional handstitching techniques to join lace and fabric panels.*

■ *Roll and whip, although quite hard to master at first, is the most important stitch in handsewing. To obtain even fabric gatherings, after every fourth stitch, push the fabric back along the tightened drawn thread. Waxing the thread with beeswax (after you've inserted the needle, but before you start sewing) strengthens the thread.*

■ *Entredeux (French for between two) fits between two pieces of rolled and whipped fabric. It has a smooth, raised right side and a rougher wrong side. Trim batiste from wrong side of entredeux before use.*

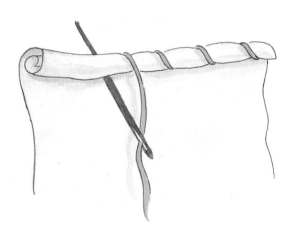

1 Draw threads at edge of cotton voile fabric to ensure it is cut on straight grain.

Cut one 22cm x 7cm fabric strip for centre panel on front of cushion.

Roll and whip hem along both long sides. Follow the diagrams above and see the Note for guidance.

Made by Sylvia Kennedy.

centre panel

2 Cut 22cm lengths of 1cm-wide lace, pink entredeux and 1.5cm-wide lace. With right sides together, whip 1cm-wide lace to rolled and whipped hem, stitching into each hole of the entredeux edging on the lace, as above.

With right sides together, whip pink entredeux to lace, again stitching into each hole.

With right sides together, whip one side of 1.5cm-wide lace to entredeux, in the same way.

pink entredeux

centre panel

3 Cut another 22cm length of pink entredeux. With right sides together, whip pink entredeux to other side of lace, following above diagram.

4 Cut 22cm x 10.5cm strip of cotton voile fabric. Roll and whip one long side of fabric. Whip hemmed side to pink entredeux, as above. Measure 3cm from rolled hem on edge of centre panel.

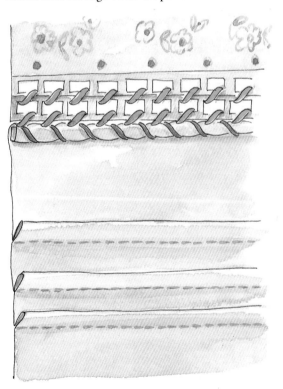

5 At this point, fold a 3mm-wide tuck. Handstitch tuck in place with small running stitches. Press tuck away from centre panel.

Measure 1.5cm from the stitching line, make

3mm tuck in the same way. Press tuck as before.

Measure 1cm from stitching line of second tuck, work another 3mm-wide tuck to give a total of three tucks, see diagram on page 97.

Work other side of panel in same way to complete front cushion. Do this by cuttting another 22cm x 10.5cm strip of cotton voile fabric. Then proceed as before to complete the third and final panel of the front of the cushion.

Embroidery: Using darker shade of silk ribbon, work a French knot in centre of panel – see photograph for position – between pink entredeux and first tuck. Using lighter shade of ribbon work stem stitches around French knot for rose petals. Using a single strand of green embroidery thread, work rose stems and leaves in straight stitch and lazy daisy stitch. For rosebuds, work a lazy daisy stitch, using lighter shade of pink silk ribbon.

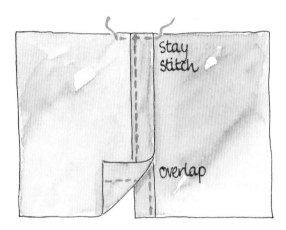

6 **Back of pillowcase:** Cut two 22cm x 18.5cm cotton voile fabric pieces.

Stitch 2cm hem on one long side of each piece.

Overlap hems by 2cm, stay stitch, see above.

Place front cushion and back cushion; right sides together. Stitch around outside edge, allowing 1cm seam allowance. Turn right side out.

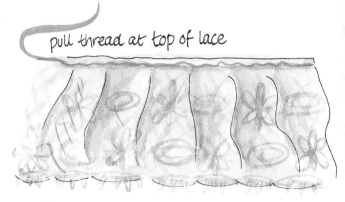

pull thread at top of lace

7 **Lace:** Pull thread in top of 3cm-wide lace to gather, pull up gathers to fit cushion, easing gathers evenly, as above. Allowing extra fullness at corners.

8 Whip gathered lace to edge of cushion, as above. Overlap ends of lace by about 5mm. Stitch down lace, press to one side, stitch flat to lace border. Fill cushion with polyester fibre filling.

Stencilling

Stencilling has been traced back as far as 500-1000 BC in China where

it appeared on silks and paper. It was carried to Europe via the trade

routes and became a favourite in the royal courts; Henry III of

England was said to be fond of gold stars stencilled on green walls. In

America, early settlers, keen to brighten their simple homes, imitated

the designs of fabrics, stencilling walls, chairs, tables and floors. The

technique is a relatively easy one involving brush, paint, pattern and a

steady hand; it remains one of the simplest ways to decorate surfaces.

You Wilil Need

Stencil paper or acetate (we used Myla)

Oil paints

Stencil brush (bristles should be a little flexible)

Saucer

Cotton buds (dab with turpentine to touch up
  rough edges of design)

Masking tape

Rubber gloves

Paper towels or newspaper

Scalpel

Ruler

Pencil

Mineral turpentine

Varnish, matt

NOTE

■ *Inspiration for stencils can be drawn from many everyday objects: fruit, flowers, trailing plants such as ivy, leaves, paper doilies, wallpaper or tapestry designs. Virtually any illustration or photograph can be converted to a stencil. For a pretty stencil, dip a length of lace in diluted varnish, allow to soak through, then hang lace up to dry.*

■ *You can cut a stencil from almost anything, but first consider its intended use. Cardboard or heavy paper can be used for small areas but the stencils will tear easily and quickly become soggy with paint. Stencil paper, semi-transparent, waxed paper is best for projects where the stencil will only be used a few times. Flexible, oiled stencil card is more durable than stencil paper but acetate is generally the material which is used most often.*

■ *Watercolour paint, felt-tip pens and crayons are not suitable for stencilling furniture, walls or floors. However, they can be used for decorating paper.*

■ *Before you begin stencilling, wipe the surface with soap and water to remove any traces of dirt, polish, varnish or grease. If there is any wax, remove it using a soft cloth which has been dipped in methylated spirits. Remove any peeling paint, if the design is to go over it.*

2 Use a cutting board or a thick layer of newspaper to protect surface of bench. Tape design in place. Carefully cut out design using a sharp scalpel or craft knife. (If cutting curves or circles, you may find it easier to rotate the design rather than the knife.)

3 Mix up paint and turpentine in saucer. Oil paint is good to use because if you make a mistake, you can wipe it off with turpentine whereas acrylic paint dries quickly and cannot always be removed successfully.

Lightly dip stencil brush into paint mixture. On a paper towel or newspaper, dab or strike the brush downward until colour is evenly distributed through brush. If you pick up too much paint on the brush at first, dab the excess onto a paper towel.

Use a separate brush for each colour.

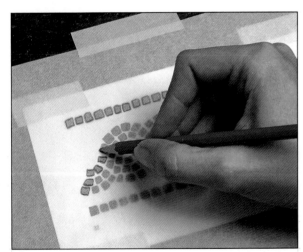

1 Tape the design onto your workbench. Place the stencil paper over the design, tape to bench. Carefully trace the design onto the paper.

Stencilling by Karen Byak.

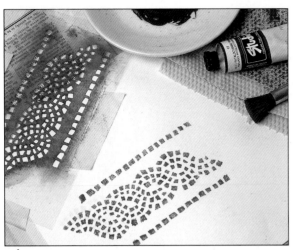

4 Perfect your technique on paper before you move on to your piece of furniture. If the pattern is to be repeated, practise lining up the design so that you get an even result.

Apply colour to exposed area of stencil in a dabbing motion, building up the colour gradually. The brush should be held upright and dabbed quickly over the design.

5 When you are satisfied with your results on paper, securely tape the stencil into position on the piece of furniture. Apply paint, carefully repeating your pattern where necessary. When complete, leave to dry (oil paint may take several days).

To protect the design from wear and tear, apply a coat of matt varnish. Make sure the stencil design has completely dried before you attempt this.

Spray paint can be used for stencilling; it gives a delicate finish with a definite edge.

Make sure to mask off the surrounding areas of the furniture with masking tape as spray paint has a tendency to spatter far and wide. Apply colour with a light hand, building up slowly. Make sure there is good ventilation in the room if you use spray paint.

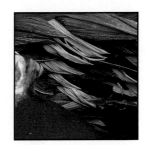

Basketwork

Basket making isn't as difficult as it looks. Traditionally the three most common types are framed (also the oldest), stake and strand, and coiled.

Our basket is an example of the latter. It is made with a central core of fibres which are then worked outwards; the coils are held in position by vertical strands called lipwork. The materials required are lightweight and easy to find, usually reflecting the vegetation of the country: willow is a popular choice in England while fine grasses feature in African baskets. We used watsonia, a plant common all over Australia.

YOU WILL NEED

4 bundles of dried watsonia (about 30 in
each bundle)

Bundle of natural raffia (available from craft
shops)

Pointed darning needle

Dried philodendron leaves, optional (about 6
or 7, we used them for decoration)

PVA glue (we used Aquadhere)

NOTE

*Gather watsonia green and hang for three weeks to dry and
shrink or, if you live in a more temperate region, pick it dry.
Dried red hot poker, bull rushes, iris or daffodil leaves all make
lovely alternatives, but you'll only get the rich bronze colour
from dried watsonia.*

1 Wrap dried watsonia overnight in a wet towel. Soaking the leaves makes coiling the basket easier.

2 Place three dampened watsonia leaves together, tie with raffia, securing with a knot. Thread darning needle with raffia.

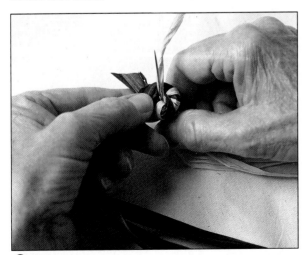

3 Conceal the raffia knot by curling the three leaves into a loop and sewing through the centre and all around the ring of leaves as shown in photograph and twisting watsonia as you go. The second row lines up behind the first row. This stitch is called 'easy stitch'.

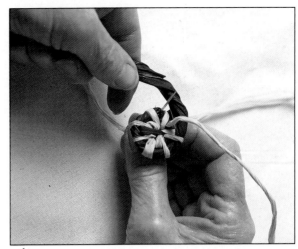

4 Roll watsonia around into a loop as you go, continue to sew with the raffia, coming up behind each row and half-way into previous row. A pattern will emerge.

When the stitches become too far apart, make a new stitch in between the existing stitch. At the same time, join in more watsonia leaves by slipping new leaves in between existing leaves (they will be secured with the raffia as you continue to stitch). Continue in this way until the base is the desired size. Finish off completely by tapering watsonia off and finishing thread by running it through watsonia.

5 Turn basket over to begin sewing on the outside, follow the line of the outside coil up until you reach the desired height. When you have wound and stitched the outer-most watsonia coil to the required depth, you can finish off the basket.

To finish off basket: To end raffia, run it along the material and tuck it in to hide the ends. Adorn basket with philodendron leaves (soaked overnight in water). Sew leaves around rim or down sides with raffia.

Leave basket in dry place for a few days. Paint with glue mixture (one part Aquadhere to 10 parts water) to preserve both the materials and colour of the basket.

Made by Robin Jeffcoat, enquiries (048) 851 534.

Decoupage

The exact origins of decoupage are unknown, however, we do have some

fine Persian and Chinese examples which date back to the early 15th

century AD. The word comes from the French, decouper, which means

to cut out; it is the art of decorating ornaments with paper cut-outs which

are placed onto objects and varnished. It was a popular hobby of ladies

in Victorian England who used it to decorate valentine cards, boxes,

screens and trays. The secret of decoupage is to achieve a perfectly

smooth finish so that the paper joins cannot be detected.

YOU WILL NEED

Timber box

Images of your choice (from magazines, art books, wrapping paper, etc.)

Small sharp scissors (cuticle scissors are easy to use)

Blu-Tack reusable adhesive

Sandpaper, very fine and medium, in several grades

Assorted brushes

Rubber roller

Steel wool

Craft knife

Sealer (we used Polyglaze)

Lead pencil

Varnish (we used Instant Estapol gloss)

PVA glue (we used Aquadhere)

Paper glue (we used Clag)

Acrylic primer paint

Wax gilt cream, optional (used for an antique finish around the lip of the box)

Artist's acrylic paints

Mineral turpentine, for cleaning brushes

NOTE

■ *It's best to work in a dust free room.*

■ *To avoid bubbles, stir the varnish, but don't shake it.*

■ *Make sure brush is free of mineral turpentine before using it to apply varnish. Varnish in one direction, and then on the next coat, work at right angles to previous direction.*

Designed and made by Stephen Westgarth. Photographed at Original Finish, Newtown, NSW.

1 Paint box with primer, allow to dry. Cut out images carefully, using sharp scissors – it is easiest to cut curves by moving the paper around the scissor blade, rather than by moving the scissors.

Arrange images on the box until satisfied with the design; consider using distant images in the background and close-ups in the foreground to give perspective and depth to the design.

2 Use small images to cover any blank areas of the box. Once satisfied with the arrangement, fix images in place temporarily with small pieces of Blu-Tack. Using a lead pencil, mark the corner positions of the main images on the surface of the box. Remove images, set aside, noting position of each.

You could make a rough sketch of the order in which you wish them to appear.

3 Mix a little paper glue with PVA glue to increase drying time. This will allow you a little extra time to position the images. It also produces a less sticky glue so you can smooth the cut-outs down.

Apply glue to box and to the wrong side of main images, beginning with the background images.

4 Place images onto the box, one at a time. When the image is glued in position, carefully brush PVA glue over its surface.

5 Gently smooth the image with a fingertip, working from the centre to the outside edge, removing any wrinkles, lumps of glue or air bubbles. If there are lumps of glue under the images, make a small cut in the image using the craft knife and release the glue.

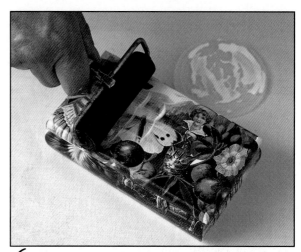

6 When all images are in place, lightly roll a roller across the surface to remove excess glue. Allow to dry.

7 Fill in any uncovered spots with artist's acrylic paints; allow to dry. Paint inside of box and any blank edges with a complementary or contrasting colour.

Apply a coat of sealer, allow to dry. (Sealing prevents show-through of images on the reverse side of paper which may happen if varnish is applied directly.) Apply varnish, allow to dry. Lightly sandpaper to remove any bubbles or brush hairs. Repeat until eight to 10 coats have been applied.

When varnish is dry, sand, using medium, then very fine sandpaper, working carefully to produce a smooth finish. For an extra fine finish, rub with steel wool. Apply another coat of varnish. When dry, sand until smooth.

Repeat process, sanding thoroughly between each coat, using a finer grade of sandpaper each time. Continue until at least another 10 coats have been applied, or until no ridges are visible around the edge of images.

Lace Making

Examples of openwork fabrics have been found in Ancient Egyptian and other Near Eastern burial sites. These fragments are possibly the forerunners of needlepoint lace. Lace as we know it, first appeared in Europe — notably Flanders and Venice — during the 15th century. It originated from embroidery. However, bobbin lace, like our handkerchief edging, evolved from weaving around a century later. It is made on a round or oval pillow and the pattern is worked with pins and thread-covered bobbins. There can be as many as 200 bobbins in one design.

YOU WILL NEED

40-50cm diameter square or circular lace pillow (you could use a 5cm thick piece of cotton-covered polystyrene)

15 pairs of bobbins (these can be made from dowelling, wooden or plastic clothes pegs, butcher's skewers, even chopsticks)

Fine pointed embroidery scissors

Good quality cardboard to put pattern on (this is called a pricking)

Clear contact to cover the pricking

0.6mm crochet hook for the sewings

Thread, DMC Special Dentelles 80 cotton or 80 linen

Stainless steel or good quality dressmaker's pins, to hold the lace in place

Finished size: Four copies of this pattern makes a handkerchief edge measuring 22.5cm x 22.5cm

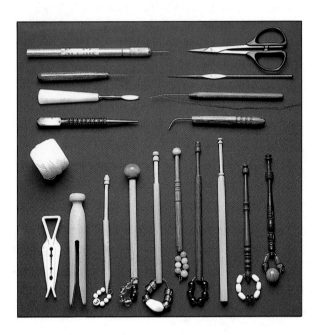

NOTE

For this project you will need to have a basic understanding of lace making skills. For further information contact the Australian Lace Guild, Inc, PO Box 609 Manly, NSW 2095. (The Guild will reside in NSW until September 1995).

Designed and made by Ethel Zuccolotto, enquiries (02) 644 9547.

---

1 Prepare the pricking (page 114). Photocopy pattern, place on cardboard and cover carefully with contact.

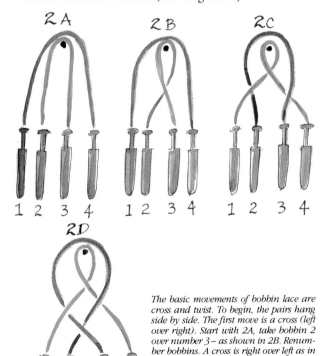

Hold bobbin in left hand, hold end of thread securely, and wind it around the bobbin away from you. When the required thread is wound on (around 3m), secure it with a hitch. Make a loop with the running end (the one leading to the ball) on the head of the bobbin, see diagram 1. Tighten the loop. Do not cut the thread, but measure out the amount required (i.e. same amount) for another bobbin. Then cut thread off at the ball. Wind this end of the thread onto another bobbin. This completes a coupled pair, see diagram 2A, below.

2 Wind and couple bobbins as in diagram 1. Diagram 2 shows how to work half stitch and cloth stitch. These are your basic stitches for bobbin lace. Workers are the pairs going across from side to side, and passives are the ones hanging straight, see diagram 3, which shows how to hang the pairs and how to start the trails.

For the outer trail: One pair of workers and five pairs of passives. (Half stitch – diagram 5 – with double stitch on outer edge – diagram 6.)

Inner trail: One pair of workers and four pairs of passives (cloth stitch – diagram 4)

Footside: Two pairs of workers and two pairs of passives (The footside is the straight edge with which the lace is mounted on fabric, see diagram 7.)

The basic movements of bobbin lace are cross and twist. To begin, the pairs hang side by side. The first move is a cross (left over right). Start with 2A, take bobbin 2 over number 3 – as shown in 2B. Renumber bobbins. A cross is right over left as in 2C. Take 2 over 1 and 4 over 3 as in 2C. Renumber bobbins.
Half stitch: b-c. See also diagram 5.
Cloth stitch: b-c-d. See also diagram 4.
Double stitch: b-c-b-c. See also diagram 6.

3 Start where the trails cross the first time, just after the corner, (marked with an X), as on the pricking.

Hang two worker pairs on two pins close together, at the top of the crossover.

3A

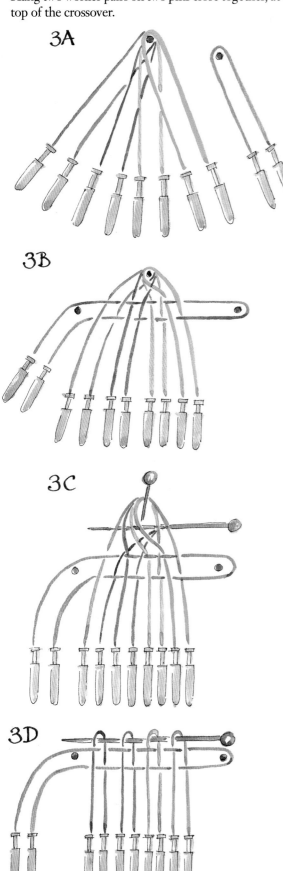

3B

3C

3D

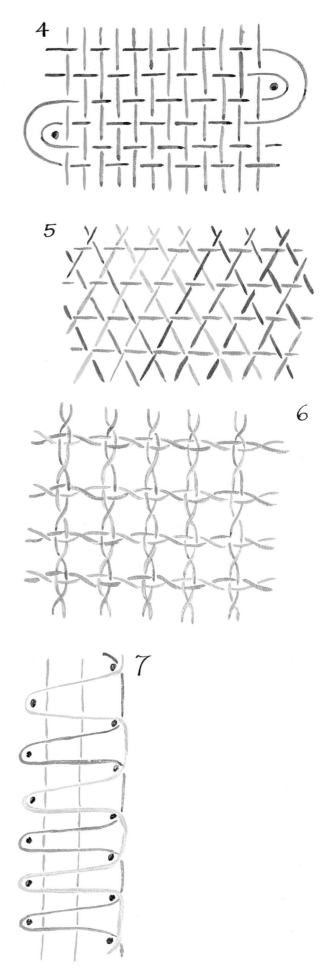

4

5

6

7

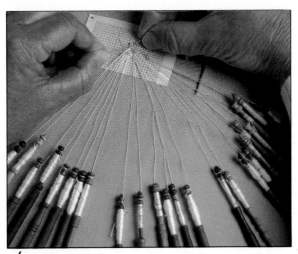

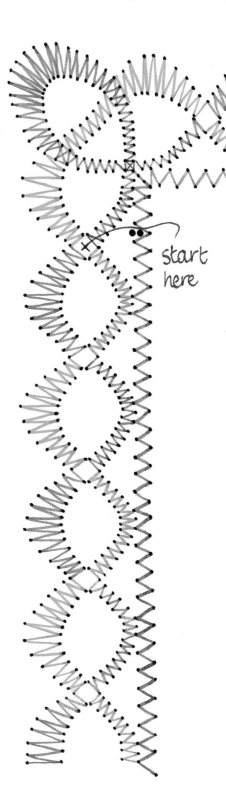
start here

4 Put in a pin on the line at each of the upper arms of the X, and hang four pairs of bobbins on each, as in diagram 3A.

Hang one pair of bobbins on a pin just above the pinhole on the left corner of the crossover (you can put the pin between the two marked pinholes, on the outside line). Work with the six left-hand pairs. The right hand pair of this group is the worker (one of the two pairs first hung).

Take the workers through the four passive pairs on the pin (cross, twist; this is shown in steps B and C of diagram 2), then double stitch (cross, twist, cross, twist – steps B and C of diagram 2), with the pair on the edge. Give the worker pair (left-hand pair) one more twist, put up the pin in the left corner of the crossover. Work another double stitch. Now, push these two pairs to the left while you lay down the pin on which the four passive pairs hang. This can be a little tricky, so take care.

5 Work steps C and D of diagram 3, by sliding a pin under the four pairs hanging on the pin, which have been worked. Raise this pin (under the four pairs) a little, and at the same time, gently pull out the pin on which the bobbins are hanging. Now lay it across behind the two pins, either side of the trail (the pin on which the workers were hung, and the pin on the outside line), and gently straighten the passives on the pin, making sure there are no large loops on the pin.

Take the other worker pair (of the first two pins), and work cloth stitch (cross, twist, cross – steps B, C and D of diagram 2) through the four pairs on the pin in the centre of the inner trail, give the worker two twists, put up the pin in the right corner of the crossover. Take the same steps as in steps C and D of diagram 3, laying down the pin with the passives on it.

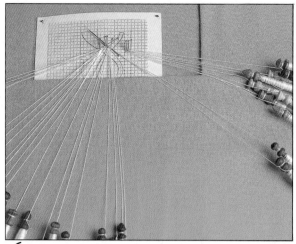

6 You will now have four pairs on each of two pins, lying across the trails. They will work cloth stitch through the other pairs (the four pairs on the left-hand side will work cloth stitch through the four pairs on the right, one pair at a time.) Number the four pairs on the left from one to four. Then, starting with number four, work through the four pairs on the right. Then work numbers three, two and one through.

The outside trail will now be worked in half stitch, with a double stitch outside edge, and the inner trail will be worked in cloth stitch to the pinhole, where the footside edge meets it.

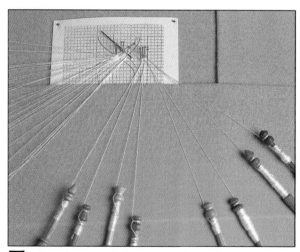

7 **For the footside edge:** Hang two pairs of workers on the pin to the right of the two small dots. These are the workers. Work double stitch with them. Twist the right-hand pair once more.

Hang one pair of passives on each of the pins placed in at the *enlarged* dots on the pricking. These are adjacent to X, where the trails cross.

Take the left-hand pair of the workers, work double stitch through the two passive pairs. Give the workers one more twist, put up the pin, double stitch through two passive pairs, put up the pin, work double stitch with the edge pair. Give the right-hand pair one more twist, see diagram 7. Repeat these moves until inner trail and footside meet.

8 When this happens, at a common pinhole, the two worker pairs (one from footside and one from trail) work double stitch, pin, double stitch. The inner trail workers are worked out and back to the pinhole between the footside pinholes. Then out to the edge, and back to work with the footside workers (which have worked to the edge, exchanged workers, and worked back), double stitch, pin, double stitch.

Repeat the above working to the crossover just before the corner.

9 Work the footside to the pinhole connecting it to the inner trail, leaving one twist only on the waiting worker pair.

Work the inner trail to the pinhole connecting it to the footside. Work the connecting pinhole.

Work the inner corner of the footside. Leave the right hand pair untwisted. Work out to the pinhole on the trail side corner. Put a pin at each of the pinholes, to keep the passives forming a neat square corner, see diagram 8.

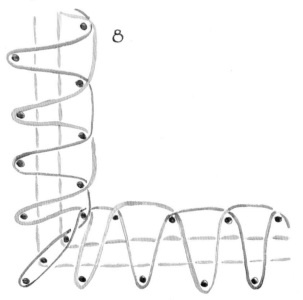

10 After working the trail side pinhole, work to the inside corner of the footside.

This pin has to be worked again. Do a double stitch with the workers. The inner trail is continued in cloth stitch, beginning at the corner loop, until the outside line of the outer trail. Now change to half stitch, with a double stitch outer edge, round to the crossover, where the trail again becomes cloth stitch. Then continue to the corner crossover. Four sewings will be taken at these four pinholes.

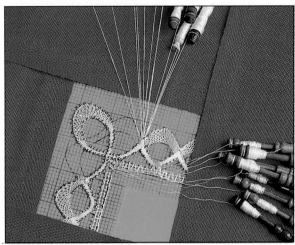

11 **To do a sewing:** Take the pin out of the hole to be sewn, insert a crochet hook through this loop, see diagram 9A, and pull one of the worker threads through to form a loop. Take the other worker bobbin through this loop, diagram 9B, then gently pull both bobbins, until the loop is closed. Replace the pin in the loop, diagram 9C. After completing these four sewings, there will be another pin to be worked with the footside and trail workers, such as was worked before the corner.

12 The outer trail works across the corner loop, continuing half stitch, sewing at the four pinholes, where the two trails cross. Before working across the loop, remove the pins that will be covered by the work; they will be too difficult to remove, once they are covered.

13 Repeat the first side three more times, to complete the handkerchief edge.

11

14 **To finish off:** Sew out each pair into its beginning loop, i.e., passives into the loops around the pins that are lying flat. Slide out the pin and sew the passives one at a time; then the edge passives, and the workers. Also sew the footside workers, and passives in a reef knot, see diagram 11, leaving a length on each to be sewn neatly along the work (for about 2cm), to secure. The trails will each be tied off in a 'grub' finish.

After all pairs in the trail have been sewn out, see diagram 10A, tie the worker pair once, then, with the left thread, tie once, in turn, with each of the passives threads, diagram 10B. When it has reached the other end, leave this thread, and tie back across all the threads, one at a time, (with the last thread tied) second from left, diagram 10C. When the right side has been reached, repeat the first row, diagram 10D. Complete the 'grub' by tying the last two threads (left-hand pair) in a reef knot. After each row, make sure all the knots are tight. Finally, cut off all threads as close to the knots as possible.

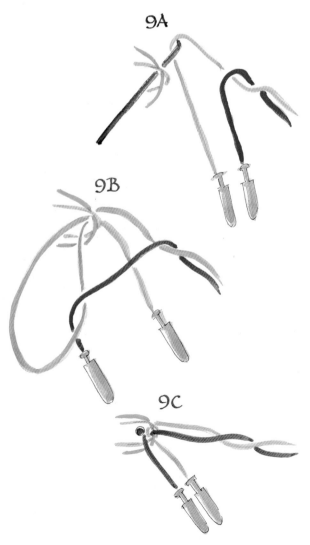

9A

9B

9C

116

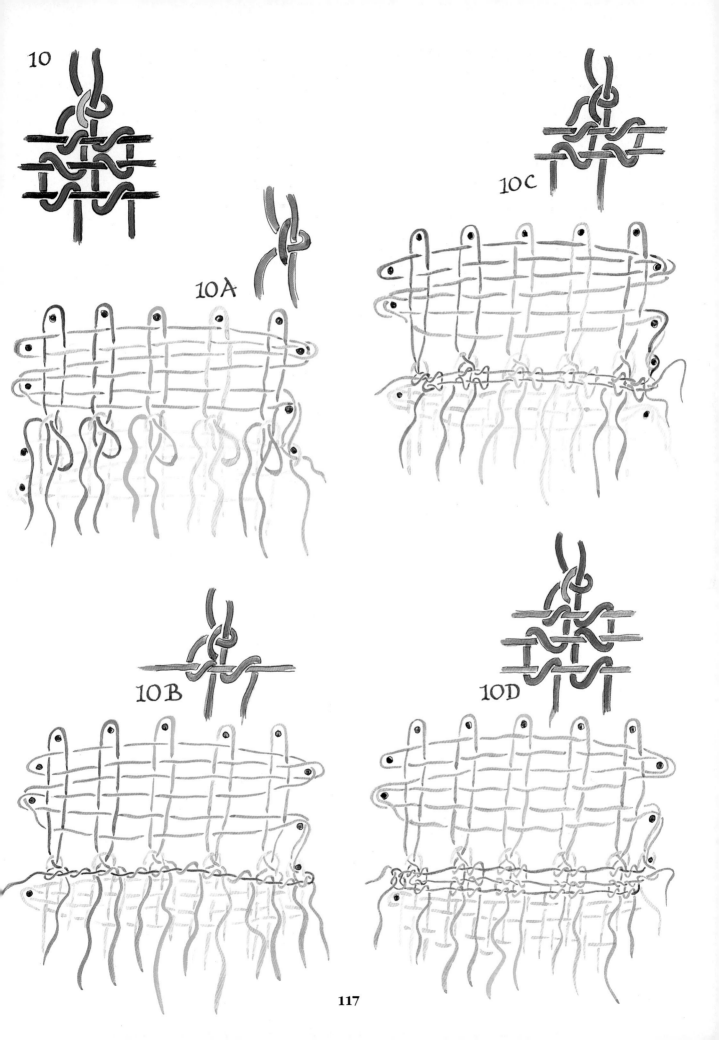

10

10A

10B

10C

10D

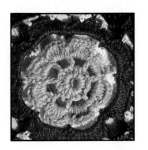

Crochet

The word crochet comes from the French, croc, which means a hook. It

is done by making a looped fabric, one stitch at a time, using a continuous

length of yarn and a hook. The art of crocheting is widely believed to

have come from North Africa. However, like so many skills, examples

can be found all over the world. For instance, nun's lace, a particularly

dainty type of crochet, first appeared in Renaissance Italy during the

16th century. Versions are also found in Spain and Ireland. The craft

probably came to Australia via the early Irish convicts.

You Will Need

Panda Regal Cotton 4 ply (50g balls)
Main Colour (MC – navy) 6 balls
First contrast (C1 – white) 5 balls
Second contrast (C2 – yellow) 6 balls
Third contrast (C3 – green) 5 balls
Fourth contrast (C4 – red) 5 balls
3.50mm crochet hook

Finished size: 150cm x120cm (approx)

Tension

One square (nine rounds) measures 10cm x 10cm on 3.50mm hook.

Abbreviations

beg=begin/ning; cm=centimetres; ch=chain; dc=double crochet; folls=follows; htr=half treble; 1p/s=loop/s; rep=repeat; rem=remaining; slst=slip stitch; st/s=stitch/es; tog=together; tr=treble.

1 Square A (See Diagram)
Using 3.50mm hook and C4, make 6ch and join with a slst to form a ring.

First Round: 1ch, (1dc, 1tr) eight times in ring, slst in first dc at beg.

Second Round: 6ch, miss 1tr, 1tr next dc, (3ch, miss 1tr, 1tr in next dc) six times, 3ch, slst in third ch at beg.

Third Round: Using C3, 1ch, (1dc, 1htr, 5tr, 1htr, 1dc) in each 3ch 1p to end, slst in first dc at beg ... eight shells.

Fourth Round: 1ch, 1dc between last dc and first dc of previous round (thus working between shells), 6ch, * 1dc between next 2 shells, 6ch, rep from * to end, slst in first dc at beg.

Fifth Round: 1ch, (1dc, 1htr, 6tr, 1htr, 1dc) in each 6ch 1p to end, slst in first dc at beg.

Sixth Round: Using C2, as fourth round.

Seventh Round: 1ch, (1dc, 1htr, 7tr, 1htr, 1dc) in each 6ch 1p to end, slst in first dc at beg. Fasten off colour in use.

Eighth Round: Join C1 with a slst in first of 7tr in first shell, 1ch, 1dc in 2nd of 7tr in shell, 6ch, miss 3tr, 1dc in next tr, (6ch, 1dc in 2nd of 7tr in next shell, 6ch, miss 3tr, 1dc in next tr) 7 times, 3ch, 1tr in first dc at beg **.

Ninth Round: Join MC with slst in top of last tr of previous round, 3ch, 3tr around stem of last tr in previous round, 4ch, 1dc in first 6ch 1p, * (6ch, 1dc in next 6ch 1p) twice, 4ch, (4tr, 4ch, 4tr) in next 6ch 1p, 4ch, 1dc in next 6ch 1p *, rep from * to * twice more, (6ch, 1dc in next 6ch 1p) twice, 4ch, (4tr, 4ch) in next 3ch 1p, slst in 3rd ch at beg.

Fasten off.

Make a further 44 squares in same manner, *omitting ninth round.*

2 Square B
Work as for Square A to **, using C2 for 6ch 1p and first three rounds, C1 for next two rounds, C4 for next two rounds and C1 for eighth round (ninth round will be worked when all of the completed squares are joined tog).

Make a further 44 squares in same manner.

3 Square C
Work as for Square A to **, using C4 for 6ch 1p and first 3 rounds, C1 for next two rounds, C3 for next two rounds and C1 for eighth round (ninth round will be worked when all of the completed squares are joined tog).

Make a further 44 squares in same manner.

4 Square D

Work as for Square A to **, using C3 for 6ch 1p and first two rounds, C2 for next three rounds, C4 for next two rounds and C1 for eighth round (ninth round will be worked when all of the completed squares are joined tog).

Make a further 44 squares in same manner.

5 To make up:

Join squares tog (noting to work out from completed square A in order indicated on joining Diagram) by working joining dcs only along edges where joins are necessary in ninth rounds of rem squares as folls – Using MC, 3ch, 3tr around stem of last tr in previous row, *** if necessary, work 1dc (joining dc) into corresponding position on previous square ***, 4ch, 1dc in first 6ch 1p, * (3ch, rep from *** to ***, 3ch, 1dc in next 6ch 1p) twice, 4ch, rep from *** to ***, (4tr, 2ch, rep from *** to ***, 2ch, 4tr) in next 6ch 1p, rep from *** to ***, 4ch, 1dc in next 6ch 1p, rep from * to * twice more, (3ch, rep from *** to ***, 3ch, 1dc in next 6ch 1p) twice, 4ch, rep from *** to ***, (4tr, 2ch, rep from *** to ***, 2ch) in next 3ch 1p, slst in 3rd ch at beg. Fasten off.

B	A	D	C	B	A	D	C	B	A	D	C	B	A	D
A	D	C	B	A	D	C	B	A	D	C	B	A	D	C
D	C	B	A	D	C	B	A	D	C	B	A	D	C	B
C	B	A	D	C	B	A	D	C	B	A	D	C	B	A
B	A	D	C	B	A	D	C	B	A	D	C	B	A	D
A	D	C	B	A	D	C	B	A	D	C	B	A	D	C
D	C	B	A	D	C	B	A	D	C	B	A	D	C	B
C	B	A	D	C	B	A	D	C	B	A	D	C	B	A
B	A	D	C	B	A	D	C	B	A	D	C	B	A	D
A	D	C	B	A	D	C	B	A	D	C	B	A	D	C
D	C	B	A	D	C	B	A	D	C	B	A	D	C	B
C	B	A	D	C	B	A	D	C	B	A	D	C	B	A

↑
First Square

KEY

⬬ = 1ch

— = sl st

+ = 1dc

𝍫 = 1tr

Τ = 1htr

✗ = Joining dc–work 1dc between sts (where indicated) into corresponding position on previous square **only along edges where joins are necessary**, *at same time* keeping patt correct in ninth round.

121

Kennedia
nigricans

Paper Making

The invention of paper making is usually attributed to Ts'ai Lun, a Chinese clerk, who in 105AD, had to find a cheaper alternative to silk as a medium for writing. Paper making eventually reached Japan, Korea and Egypt, where a much thicker paper using cotton cloth was made. This Egyptian style of paper making gradually spread across Europe and then to America. By the 18th century, a cheaper, raw material was needed to satisfy demand. Wood is still used as a basic raw material. However, hemp and flax are often used for better quality paper.

You Will Need

Mould and deckle (specialist equipment, contact your state's Crafts Council for information on local suppliers)

Large rectangular container, to hold mould and deckle (a plastic storage container, baby's bath or kitchen sink will do)

Scrap paper, must be at least 10cm wider all around than mould and deckle (do not use newsprint or plastic-coated paper)

Bucket

Drill with metal paint stirrer (blender or food processor can substitute)

Squares of linen or other fabric, for the couching cloth which determines the texture of the paper (use hessian for a rough texture)

2cm thick sponge, same size as mould

Paper press (a paper press can be made with two boards and two or four G-clamps to hold boards tightly together; a book press or heavy bricks can also be used)

2 boards, extra

Note

■ *Mould: Can be made at home using a small picture or window frame with fabric stretched tautly across it. Alternatively, use a small silk-screen.*

■ *Deckle: This is a wooden frame the same shape and size as mould. Finished paper will be this size too.*

1 Tear paper into 3.5cm squares, soak in warm water in a bucket for several hours. If you use boiling water, the process will only take about 30 minutes.

2 Pulverise the paper squares with metal paint stirrer for about 15 minutes or until fibres separate. Pulp should be an even consistency, like whipped cream, without any large pieces of paper.

For smaller quantities, a blender or food processor can be used.

Pour warm water and three cups of pulp into large container, stir until pulp is evenly distributed.

3 Holding the mould and deckle so the deckle does not slip, dip into the container and gently slide to the bottom until lying flat.

6 Rock mould back and forth until paper has stuck to the couching cloth; carefully lift off mould.

4 Slowly bring mould and deckle out of the container, keeping mould horizontal and gently shake it from side to side until most of the water has drained out. Drain off excess water by tilting towards one corner.

7 **To emboss paper:** Place a leaf, flower, lace or any thin, textured object onto sheet of wet paper in desired position. Cover with another piece of damp couching cloth. A stack of eight to 10 sheets can be made by placing a piece of couching cloth between each sheet.

5 Put damp couching cloth on sponge, remove deckle and place the mould face down on couching cloth.

8 Place sheets with damp couching cloth in paper press (best results are obtained with heavy pressure).

9 After one hour, remove clamps and carefully lift each couching cloth.

10 To dry, hang paper sheet and couching cloth on a line indoors. When paper is nearly dry, carefully pull it off couching cloth, remove item used for embossing and press paper between two dry boards.

Envelopes: Open out a ready-made envelope and use as a pattern to cut handmade paper. Fold and glue envelope together.

Handmade Cards

Beautiful cards can be made from recycled paper and natural plant materials. The colour of the handmade paper will depend upon the colour of the paper it is made from. Cards can be decorated with pressed flowers and leaves.

YOU WILL NEED

Handmade paper
Dried flowers and leaves
Glue stick
PRESSING FLOWERS
Freshly picked flowers and leaves, pickflowers which have just opened, (flat and small flowers and leaves press well)
Flower press (heavy books will do)
Thick white blotting paper
Thin sheets of cardboard, same size as paper
Soft brush
Adhesive tape

NOTE

■ *Large or flowers with many petals, such as roses, will need to be gently pulled apart and each petal pressed separately. Daffodils can be cut in half. If flowers have large seed pods attached, these should be removed before pressing. All flowers should be pressed separately from their stems and leaves. Likewise, stem and leaf shape can change dramatically during pressing, so choose flowers carefully.*

■ *As colours fade, it's best to use brightly coloured flowers like pansies and violets to obtain good results.*

■ *Everlasting flowers are also good to press and keep their colour well.*

Handmade cards: Carefully fold sheets of hand-made paper in half.

Position card so it opens from the right. Decorate the card by arranging pressed flowers or leaves on front in an interesting design. Glue in place. See instructions for pressing flowers below.

Draw a border with black or contrasting coloured pen, if desired. For envelopes, see instructions for hand-made paper, page 126.

Pressing flowers: Using a soft brush, arrange flowers face down on blotting paper. Touch flowers as little as possible to avoid damaging them. Make sure flowers do not touch each other.

Tape stems to the paper.

Cover flowers with blotting paper, then with cardboard. A number of layers can be sandwiched together in this way.

If using a flower press, screw press together as tightly as possible. As flowers settle, tighten the press again. Be careful with delicate flowers because too much pressure will damage them.

If a press is unavailable, flowers may be pressed within a book or between heavy books. Leave book in a dry place for a day. Transfer flowers to fresh pieces of blotting paper and press for another two days. Flowers can be left for longer; the longer they are left the better the preserved colour will be.

If flowers are not required immediately, store them in a heavy book with blotting paper, well out of the light.

Made by Gail Stiffe.

Index